CHASING

DOWN

A RUMOR

The Death of Mainline
Denominations

Robert Bacher and Kenneth Inskeep

Augsburg Books
MINNEAPOLIS

CHASING DOWN A RUMOR
The Death of Mainline Denominations

Large-quantity purchases or custom editions of this book are available at a discount from the publisher. For more information, contact the sales department at Augsburg Fortress, Publishers, 1-800-328-4648, or write to: Sales Director, Augsburg Fortress, Publishers, P. O. Box 1209, Minneapolis, MN 55440-1209.

Library of Congress Cataloging-in-Publication Data
Bacher, Robert.
  Chasing down a rumor : the death of mainline denominations / Robert Bacher and Kenneth Inskeep.
     p. cm.
  Includes bibliographical references (p.   ).
  ISBN 0-8066-5142-3 (pbk. : alk. paper)
  1. Protestant churches—United States. 2. United States—Church history—20th century.
I. Inskeep, Kenneth, 1953- II. Title.
  BR526.B25 2005
  280'.4'0973—dc22   2005002347

Excerpt from "The Church of Christ in Every Age" by Fred Pratt Green, © 1971 Hope Publishing Co., Carol Stream, IL 60188. All rights reserved. Used by permission.

Cover design by Diana Running, cover art from PhotoDisc.
Book design by Michelle L. N. Cook.

The paper used in this publication meets the minimum requirements of American National Standard for Information Sciences—Permanence of Paper for Printed Library Materials, ANSI Z329.48-1984. ♾ ™

Manufactured in the U.S.A.

09   08   07   06   05   1   2   3   4   5   6   7   8   9   10

CONTENTS

"The report of my death was an exaggeration."
—Mark Twain
New York Journal
June 2, 1897

"The Church of Christ, in ev'ry age
Beset by change, but Spirit-led
Must claim and test its heritage
And keep on rising from the dead."
—Fred Pratt Green
Lutheran Book of Worship, 433

ACKNOWLEDGMENTS

We have borrowed from many people in writing this book. Some we can remember in addition to those persons we have cited in the references and footnotes.

First, there is the group of denominational administrators who has been meeting since 1992 to share ideas, experiences, frustrations, and especially to encourage each other. The "dis-connect" between the Rumor and actual experience was often "felt" in being part of this group. The two of us began to write and speak about it, expanding our thoughts as we went, trying to make sense of what mainlines were actually going through. Soon we had a book.

Second, we have learned much from religious researchers, some in denominational offices and others who teach in colleges or seminaries. These researchers provided us with their studies and reports, and we deeply appreciate it. Their work has helped to shape this book, although we can guarantee they will not agree with everything we have done with their work!

Third, we are grateful to the leaders and members of our denomination, the Evangelical Lutheran Church in

America (ELCA). In congregations, synods, the national office (called the churchwide organization, not exactly an exotic title!), and in church-related organizations, these five million people seek each day to faithfully and effectively carry out ministry and mission that is born neither of denial of challenges nor despair about the future. In the ELCA national office, you will find, as have we, the most committed, hardworking, and competent people anywhere. Each denomination has them. Someone should study their motivation. Why do they do this work? From them we have received encouragement and inspiration.

The results of the interviews conducted for this book show up primarily in chapters 5 and 6. To those who shared their time, expertise, insights, and denominational material, we express our appreciation.

The authors of a book need many partners. We thank Nancy Vaughn, who also typed portions of the manuscript. At Augsburg Fortress, Publishers, we would like to thank Beth Lewis, Scott Tunseth, and Michelle L. N. Cook.

We reserve the final expression of gratitude to our families. Thank you for the patient questions ("Is the book finished yet?"), love, and support. Our spouses, Shirley and Jackie, were especially helpful in reading the manuscript, making suggestions along the way, believing it could be done, and providing encouragement when it was needed most. To them we dedicate this book. We also want to acknowledge the help of John Hessian.

Finally, God does not need mainline denominations. We pray, however, that God will keep and use them for God's purposes and work. To God be the glory!

FOREWORD

I n 1950, when the National Council of Churches announced its plans to construct a building that would house the offices of America's mainline Protestant denominations, the editors of *Christian Century*, the flagship magazine for liberal Protestantism, implored the Council not to locate the building in Manhattan. The editors pointed out that Protestantism was a minority faith in New York City, and if Protestant leaders were serious about tapping into "the psychological center of its constituency to insure the maximum response to its leadership," they should look elsewhere. Readers agreed, flooding the magazine with suggestions for alternative sites, including Minneapolis, Chicago, St. Louis, Kansas City, and Wichita. One reader suggested "the southeastern part of Nebraska," and another opined that Manhattan, Kansas, would be more fitting than Manhattan, New York.

The National Council of Churches ignored those suggestions, however, and proceeded with the construction of the Interchurch Center on the upper west side of Manhattan. President Dwight D. Eisenhower laid the cornerstone for the International Style building on October 12, 1958, offering paeans to America's religious character.

Shortly thereafter, however, at least according to most indices of membership, attendance, and giving, the fortunes of mainline Protestantism began to decline. Many observers have offered various reasons for this: the rise of the counterculture, the activism of denominational leaders in the civil rights and anti-Vietnam War movements, the religious indifference of the baby boom generation, the resurgence of evangelicalism, perhaps even the geographical distance between Protestant leaders and their constituents. In the course of my travels in the early 1990s to revisit the twelve "great churches" so designated by *Christian Century* in 1950, I found still other reasons for concern. In Orlando, Florida, for instance, the congregation of the First United Methodist

Church had made a principled decision in the 1950s to remain downtown, even as most of its congregants fled to the suburbs and eventually into the waiting arms of evangelical megachurches.

While mainline Protestantism has doubtless been buffeted by cultural, political, and demographic changes over the last several decades, this remarkable book offers persuasive evidence that, recalling the famous Peace Corps ads of the 1960s, the glass is half full rather than half empty. Kenneth Inskeep and Robert Bacher acknowledge that mainline Protestantism has fallen on hard times, but they insist that rumors of its imminent demise are greatly exaggerated. Commendably, after debunking the rumor, the authors take the argument one step further. "We want to see renewed confidence, even audacity," they write, "particularly among mainline clergy and others who work so diligently toward making the world a better place in the name of Jesus."

This message comes at a propitious moment in our history. There can be little question, especially after the election of 2004, that the Religious Right has seized center stage as the primary religious voice in American public discourse, becoming in the process an echo chamber for the platform of the Republican Party. Tragically, in so doing, the Religious Right has defaulted on the noble legacy of nineteenth-century evangelical activism, which invariably took the part of those on the margins of society—slaves, women, and the poor. I find little resemblance between the evangelical reformers of the antebellum period and the culture warriors of the Religious Right, and the tragedy deepens when one considers that, because of the Religious Right's media presence and its savvy political alliances, it is virtually the only voice—and it is certainly the loudest voice—invoking the language of faith.

Many Americans now openly yearn for the rebirth of the so-called Religious Left, and this book provides the basis for a new confidence on the part of mainline Protestants. Although there is serious work to be done in the way of careful theological thinking and connecting with constituents, mainline Protestants should be relieved to learn that their plight is not as bad as many have led them to believe. That is not so say that mainline Protestants should expend all of their capital on political matters—or that their positions should invariably skew toward the left—but it is high time that mainline Protestants reclaim their voice on matters of consequence for the faith, for the church, for the nation, and for the world.

Chasing Down a Rumor should help them do just that.

—*Randall Balmer*

INTRODUCTION

*They have survived. Even parachurch groups work
with the loyalties and member lists of denominations.*
—Martin Marty, 1991

*The denomination, unlike the traditional forms of
the church, is not primarily confessional, and it is
certainly not territorial. Rather it is purposive.*
—Sidney Mead, 1963

T his is an essay on the *duration* of the church.
More accurately, it is a set of observations about
the endurance of a fundamentally American
form of the church: the mainline denomination.

What follows is an examination of mainline
denominations on the heels of an already long list of
popular musings and serious studies. Many have analyzed the past and speculated about what's next for the
mainline. We believe we have something different to
offer. We serve notice that we are not dispassionate
bystanders. One of us is recently retired after spending

most of a lifetime working for the national office of a mainline denomination; the other currently spends his days working in that same office. We believe in mainline denominations. We believe that mainline denominations serve as caretakers of a wonderfully important American expression of the Christian faith and that if they are weak or lost, American society and the universal church will be the worse for it. We believe that no other American institutions can replace them. No other segment of the society, religious or otherwise, is as concerned about, or can as readily provide the basis for, what we call an "American Community."

We are well aware that our insider status and lack of "objectivity" could lead to being dismissed. We hope you, the reader, will hang in there with us as we present our reasons why we think the rumor about mainlines is misleading. But, as for objectivity, we have often sensed that others have also been less than objective about mainline denominations. Some write with caring and even sympathy, while others find it difficult to hide their preferences for other, usually more conservative, religious institutions.

In other words, everyone has a point of view. Ours is that there is much of value in mainline denominations, and we intend to give them every benefit of the doubt. We want to hold up these traditions that have always taken the world into account. We want to give them every chance. If they have faded, we want them restored. We want to see renewed confidence, even audacity, particularly among mainline clergy and others who work so diligently toward making the world a better place in the name of Jesus. Yet, despite all this, we will do our best to keep our eyes, ears, and minds open to reality.

The Rumor

Over the last decade, a rumor has been making the rounds that mainline denominations in the United States are dying. This book chases down that rumor and, at the very least, gives it a different spin. We begin from the premise that many good rumors are based in fact, or a particular version of the facts, but we call for caution and a bit of skepticism that The Rumor has got it "right." Our alternate reading goes like this: If mainline denominations are in trouble, religion in America is in trouble. The stakes are higher than The Rumor lets on. It is worth taking a slower and more deliberate look at what we think we know. We want to make sure we understand what is underneath and around The Rumor. If we can think clearly about it, perhaps we can more effectively shape a future that is more hopeful, without being blind to the challenges.

The Rumor makes certain claims. Let's look at four of them, then examine six versions of The Rumor: "The End of Christendom," "The Death of the Church," "Right Around the Corner," "Back to the Glory Days," "A New Apostolic Age," and "A Renewal Movement from Within."

Claim One: Mainline Sidelined

The mainline has been moved to the sideline. This claim, of course, plays off the term *mainline.* When tied to falling statistics about membership and financial giving, the argument can be made that the mighty ones have been displaced from the centers of power and influence they once enjoyed. As a result, the specter of decline or even demise raises its ugly head and the fretting begins.

The label mainline stems from a period in American history, roughly 1930 to 1960, when fortified by a seemingly endless growth in members and money, certain denominations did seem to occupy a central place in American society. They were seen as the norm of what it meant to be religious in America. Other religious groups had to position themselves accordingly. That time has passed. Now pluralism is center stage for religious groups and society as a whole. The mainlines must adjust to the changed situation, and we will present evidence that shows they already have. Our objection is that the observation of being sidelined should not be taken as proof of decline or imminent death. We object on two grounds. First, the denominations labeled mainline were "up there" or "in the middle" not because they coveted center stage but because they had taken on a great dream—creating what we call the American Community. We explore this at length in chapter 3.

It didn't work, but they tried. A fall from the heights is a fall, but let's give them some credit for pursuing a society of peace and justice. Second, is a displacement from mainline to sideline a bad thing? Rather than fuel The Rumor, it can be welcomed as an opportunity to serve in a new and courageous way. We cannot but think of the writing of Dietrich Bonhoeffer as he called the Confessing Church in Nazi Germany to faithful and courageous witness precisely because that church had the illusion of privilege and power stripped away. In contemporary parlance, he shouted, "Wake up! It's a chance to serve." His actual words were, "We see from below" (Bonhoeffer, 1991:268).

Claim Two: Lights Out in 2046?

The mainlines won't survive the present statistical trends. From researchers who ought to know better, The Rumor takes assurance that the mainlines will die in the near future if the straight-line projections run their course. A speaker at one church meeting predicted that the church we know best, the Evangelical Lutheran Church in America, will "turn out the lights" in 2046.

Some trends *are* alarming: declining membership (although those declines have slowed for almost all mainlines); a loss of young people; the aging of the remaining members; and the preference for individualistic, consumeristic forms of religion over establishment traditions. As much as possible should be done to stem the tide of those trends.

Not so fast, we caution. Much of the decline-and-demise literature uses 1965—when denominations were still riding high in money and members—as a baseline year. That was the perspective behind *Newsweek*'s August 9, 1993, article "Dead-end for the Mainline? The mightiest Protestants are running out of money, members, and meaning." But there was a lot of American church history before 1965, and it's helpful to take a longer view. It shows changes that reflect trends in birth rates and immigration. It shows an ebb and flow. Straight-line projections from some earlier starting points would have wrongly predicted the deaths of some mainline bodies shortly after the founding of the Republic. In chapters 2, 3, and 4, we offer a longer view from a historic and statistical perspective.

Claim Three: Who Needs 'Em Anyway?

The mainlines are so consumed with self-preservation that they have ceased (or soon will) doing anything useful or offering anything anybody wants or needs. The Rumor rarely credits the mainlines with doing much that's good. The implication is that although they're dying, there's little reason to lament their passing. But is that claim true? It certainly isn't from an international perspective. The many projects related to hunger, injustice, development, partnership with indigenous churches, and peace-building around the world rely heavily on technical support, funding, and spiritual accompaniment from the mainlines. Most of this generous flow of support comes from individuals, congregations, middle judicatories such as synods and dioceses, and the national expression all working together. Last year, in the ELCA, $28 million was contributed and spent as part of the denomination's global mission program. That money went for food, development programs, missionaries, scholarships, and so on. It may be a drop in the bucket compared to federal government aid, much less the scope of the need, but it was the church and its caring in the name of Jesus that moved people to give for others they know very little about except that they are "brothers and sisters in Christ."

Nearly $20 million was contributed to start new congregations and revitalize existing ones in the United States as part of the domestic outreach program, and $5 million was spent to supplement pension and health care benefits for retired clergy, most of whom were inadequately compensated during their working years. Giving, in order to alleviate world hunger, has risen from $12 million per year to $16 million over the last several years.

These amounts represent over three-fourths of the money managed by what the ELCA sometimes calls its national expression. Examples from other mainlines would be similar. If the national expression of the ELCA was so intent on self-preservation, why did it pass three-fourths of its budget along to *other* ministries in the United States and around the world? Part of the remaining one-fourth of the budget supports the staff who do the work necessary to carry out mission and ministry worldwide. Said church historian Martin Marty (1991), "Even parachurch groups work with the loyalties and member lists of denominations."

Claim Four: Liberalism's the Problem
The mainlines ended up in this pickle because they are too liberal. Some of the writing on the demise of the mainlines scarcely disguises its glee in announcing the impending denominational funerals. They're apparently eager to replace us with some version of themselves—usually some more independent, loose affiliation of congregations with a conservative agenda.

The first and most sophisticated rendition of the charge that mainlines are losing ground because they have turned away from what matters most to ordinary people is offered by Dean Kelley (1972). (See chapter 3 for more detail.) His study of the success of the "strict" churches should be taken seriously. But even some nonmainline denominations are undergoing some of the changes used by The Rumor to document the decline and decay of the mainlines. For example, *Christianity Today* (February 2003) reports that the Moody Bible Institute, in an attempt to stabilize its own finances, will stop publishing *Moody Magazine,* published since 1900, because they can no longer afford to subsidize it. Moody also closed its retail stores and restructured its aviation educational program. *Christianity Today* (May 2003) also reports significant cuts (thirty-four people laid off and another sixty-six positions not filled) at Focus on the Family, "The ministry cut this year's $130 million budget by $5 million after showing a $7 million deficit in fiscal 2000." The Billy Graham Evangelistic Association "saw a $20 million giving decline, from $107 million to $87 million, from 2000 to 2001." Finally, World Vision's budget fell short by $2 million in 2002. We take no comfort in those announcements. Our point is that the plight of denominations in the United States today often has little or nothing to do with being liberal, conservative, or something in between, and that many of us are experiencing the same forces. We question the liberal-conservative labeling of whole denominations and suggest that differences within denominations are the growing challenge (see chapter 4).

These are four claims of The Rumor. For each, we offer a direct response or an alternative reading of the facts. We turn now to the major versions of The Rumor.

Metamorphoses of The Rumor

Sorting through the literature, the interviews we conducted for this project, and our personal experiences, we developed a list of the variations on The Rumor that depict life in the mainline in the worst of times. We will comment on these variations and in so doing try to show The Rumor's shortcomings while we search for a different, more productive approach.

The End of Christendom

Christendom usually refers to a period of church history that began in the reign of the Emperor Constantine. Although officially licensing a new cult, Constantine went way beyond that in establishing favorable conditions for Christianity. With his own conversion to Christianity, he declared himself to be a soldier of the Cross. He went from "protector to proselyte of the Church" initiating a whole new cycle of historical development by sponsoring the project of a Christian empire (Cochrane, 1957:183). Through a series of edicts, including the Edict of Milan in 313, Constantine protected Christians from persecution. Eventually, Christianity became the official religion, and its power was buttressed through the force of the government, including the use of violence. When Christendom ended is a matter of debate and beyond the purpose of this book. More pertinent is that some advocates of The Rumor use "the end of Christendom" as a label or metaphor for understanding the changed situation of the mainlines, especially since the 1960s.

Christendom, at least in the United States, is defined by "an informal but fully operational religious establishment"; mission work to "those far-off pagan lands"; congregations as territorial parishes encompassing the already converted; attempts to rebuild "one" unified church; and lay persons who were "loyal citizens of the realm, expected to be obedient to the powers, to pay their dues to church and state, and not bother their heads too much about theological matters." In that Christendom, being a good Christian was "identical with being a good, law-abiding, tax-paying, patriotic citizen" (see Mead, 1991:15–22).

The "end of Christendom" means that "our task is no less than the reinvention of the church" (Mead, 1991:43). "We are at the front edges of the greatest transformation of the church that has occurred for 1,600 years. It is by far the greatest change that the church has ever experienced in America; it may eventually make the transformation of the Reformation look like a ripple in a pond" (Mead, 1991:68). According to this version of The Rumor, we are in the midst of a new reformation that will see the reinvented church transformed at its "very core."

What are we to expect of this new reinvented church? What will be its form? The Rumor holds that this new church will be congregationally based with the laity playing a larger role. It will focus on local mission. It will not lose sight of its fundamental foreignness in a society and culture that it used to call home. Denominations will be of little use because "for the most part, their downward spiral has become irreversible." "A new breed of change agents . . . made up of entrepreneurial organizations and talented consultants" will step forward to help (Mead, 1991:67). What will be their strategy? What will these new entrepreneurs do? One of the primary strategies will be to focus on "learning point" congregations. The "new" strategies also include encouraging innovation and paying attention to any barriers to participation. Systems of accountability between congregations and "those who assist them in mission" should also be established. Bridges should be built. New allies should be sought. Failure should be valued—except in the case of the old, dying congregations. (See Mead, 1991:69–83.) These are all good suggestions even though we can repeatedly point to many instances where they have already been tried with very limited success even by competent outsiders.

For example, mainline denominations tried those strategies throughout much of the 1990s, but they faced formidable challenges. The transformation of a single congregation might be achievable on occasion, but transferring that learning from one congregation to another is a complex and difficult matter. Every situation is unique, and there is no evidence we know of where independent consultants succeed on a regular basis anymore than persons who work for denominations. Many congregations don't want to learn something new, because they are content with their old ways. Some congregations have to be convinced they should work together for the common good, and when it involves sacrificing their own future for the benefit of others, there are serious limits to what will be given away. In the ELCA, congregational capital expenditures, endowments, and cash on hand have risen in direct proportion to the decline for support of mission work carried out by the synods and the national office. In general, congregations are turning inward.

Most of this talk about transformation and a new reformation, how-ever, is a problem in at least two other important ways. First, this new, reinvented church appears closer to the older, well-established forms of American religion than to anything really new or different. Those older forms were built on congregationalism and individualism, and so are the "new" forms. It was the mainlines' attempt to find an "American Community" that was truly new, but the experiment failed. The challenge is not to go back but to go forward and try again.

Second, The Rumor unrealistically assumes that congregations can become something *other* than what they are on a scale that's large enough to make a difference. We would rather they become *more fully who they already are*. That's a subtle but important distinction that is being lost on the majority of mainline congregations. Put another way, it's difficult to make loyal, long-time, set-in-their-ways Lutherans, Presbyterians, Methodists, or Episcopalians anything but mainliners, and we shouldn't want to try. Instead, we want them to see themselves as part of a signifi-cant and unique expression of the universal church. They need to (re)build from their theological core, shedding some dated and corrosive cultural trappings. All congregations should not be turned into large, entrepreneurial churches. These churches have their place, but they are not enough, nor are they the only "successful" alternative. The society needs local, viable, community-based congregations that understand their local mission as part of the global church. Anything less sells them short.

The Death of the Church

This form of The Rumor holds that the entire system of the institutional church is going through a radical change and "breaking under incredible stress." The church is moving "rapidly toward a moment of decision, a defining moment." The church can or will die "because of our hidebound resistance to change, . . ." and it is on that "direct course." "If the institu-tional church does nothing, which it is in fact good at doing, the choice has been made." But, "the invisible church of Jesus Christ exists outside of and independent from the culture" (Regele, 1995:37).

From a theological perspective, the church of Jesus Christ is never tied to any particular institutional form, healthy or not. The church is always more and less than what can be seen or evaluated by The Rumor—or this book. However, the assertion that it should die so that something new may emerge is a bad one for two reasons. First, since its inception, the church has never died. It has changed, adopted, and adapted new forms and strategies over time, but not died. What would the death of the church mean? Let God handle matters of life and death. What we can do is realistically appraise the situation and try faithful, hopeful, and courageous actions, learn from them, and try again.

Second, calling for the death of the church undermines those who have worked so hard for the last five decades. We worry that the decline-and-death literature will become a self-fulfilling prophecy for the mainline denominations. Having announced the death of the church, are we implying or do we really believe there is little worth saving? Much of the analysis behind this version of The Rumor is helpful, especially for getting the attention of denominational leaders. (See Regele, 1995:55ff.) For example, "thousands of churches across America" are old or dying. "In many churches, the average age of its members is between sixty-five and seventy. More and more churches can no longer financially support themselves, and they will not recover." There is little doubt that renewing stagnant congregations should be a top priority of mainlines.

Dealing with aging congregations is a sensitive matter. Most mainline denominations do not have the authority at their national or middle expressions to close congregations at will. It wouldn't be a good idea anyway. There are, however, an increasing number of these congregations that are working together in a variety of cooperative alliances, aided by help from their denominations. Without denominational staff to help facilitate these conversations, they would be much less likely to take place. The quality of cooperation among congregations has reached a point to warrant study and documentation by theologians and sociologists. One excellent study is *Cooperating Congregations: Portraits of Mission Strategies* (Waldkoenig and Avery, 1999). The mainlines have not been asleep at the wheel about the viability of their congregations. The key, we believe, is for congregations to reappropriate their past in new and creative ways including partnerships. New ways of living out their mission can be formed from within the context of their identity as mainline churches.

Right Around the Corner

Another rendition of The Rumor holds that mainline denominations may be in ill health, but the cure is right around the corner. Keep working and maybe the members will come along. Most of the mainline denominations have repeatedly attempted evangelism campaigns. But, after years, the overall membership languishes. Why? In the "learnings" section of a recent evaluation report on the 1991–2001 ELCA Evangelism Strategy, it's reported that "many ELCA congregations were not ready to do evangelism and some did not want to become ready."[1] What did the denominational professionals do? "We shifted from primarily providing resources to increasing training events that included resources and networking. We also began providing grants for local synodical/congregational activities. In addition, we used a 'from the field to the field' strategy for providing effective evangelism models, using practitioners to share their ministry and working models with the whole church."

Did it work? Well, the losses have slowed. The truth is that denominational professionals can only try, learn, and try again, hoping they will find an answer. Their resources are limited, even as they try to refocus those resources so that they are used most effectively and efficiently. Who gets the grant money? Mostly the congregations that ask for it. How many congregations ask for it? Not nearly enough. Why? Most congregations are ambivalent about growth. Can the denominational professionals change that? They keep trying. As we have noted, old-time, loyal Lutherans are not about to turn into conservative evangelical-styled witnesses. If the denominational professionals can be faulted, it is for their inability to excite or engage the members in a mission that reaches out and is at the same time distinctly Lutheran, Presbyterian, or Methodist. Years have been spent emphasizing similarities, not differences.

We would be the first to admit that continuing down the current path, even with a strong(er) commitment to do "it" better, deeply discounts the challenges of the current context, both inside and outside of the church. Organization literature makes a distinction between doing things right and doing the right things. Doing the same things better is helpful if they are the right things.

The major premise of this book is that mainline denominations will get better if they do things that fulfill their mission purposes within the framework of their long and well established and clearly articulated identities. They should do things that express their unique character. Put another way, mainline denominations should do things that no one else could, or would, in the same way.

Back to the Glory Days

Among many dedicated church workers, but even more among the rank and file, there is a version of The Rumor that with a big push in evangelism, stewardship, and a rediscovery of the old forms of worship, the glory days will return. The glory days usually refer to the 1950s, when the mainlines were growing both in members and money. At the synod assemblies of the ELCA in 2002, for example, the voting members pointed to secularization, the decline of the family, and the corrosive forces of the mass media as the primary culprits responsible for decline.[2] These active members of the church appear to want more traditional evangelism programs (even though they are unlikely to participate themselves). They seem to want the church to "return" to its heritage and liturgical forms of worship. They talk about a return to the "Word." They think about the past when they contemplate the future. They are nostalgic about the 1950s. They seem unhappy that the world has moved on and they look to the national denominational offices to stage a "comeback," one they long for but feel powerless to affect. Instead, the rank and file often see the national denominational office as part of the problem, not the solution.

We suggest thinking about the past as we contemplate the future, but not a longing for the past. Instead, we ask, "What does the tradition tell us about the core of a mainline religious identity and how can it be used to make the world a better place in the here and now?" None of the "problems" often associated with secularization, changes in the family, or the media are going to go away, but the genius of the mainline is its ability to live in the world without losing sight of how much better the world could be.

A New Apostolic Age

A fifth expression of The Rumor is that denominations will be rendered excess baggage with the dawning of a "new apostolic age." This is an attractive argument, but deceptive. Its attraction lies in the desire for a time, namely, of the New Testament and first several centuries, when the Christian message was being spread across the known world with great power and courage. To read the New Testament's Acts of the Apostles is to be placed in the presence of story after story of those who not only heard the message but carried it forth in wonderful ways, often at great personal risk. Who would not long for such a time to be repeated? The promise of the Holy Spirit's guidance and inspiration, however, is given to the church, in the words of the hymn quoted at the beginning of this book, "in ev'ry age." To long for a *then,* even such a powerful one, seems an avoidance of responsibility *now.* And, of course, there is all the history and witness of faithful persons between the Apostolic Age and today. The wish for a presumably purer world and more powerful period runs roughshod over twenty-one centuries of God's work among us.

In addition, the proponents of this new apostolic age see the original congregations spread across the Roman Empire as a loose connection of congregations remarkably like a new, contemporary network of autonomous congregations. In other words, what is wanted for the present time is "read" back into Apostolic time. This "network" view declares the modern denomination a mistake and discredits the role denominations have played. The history of the church from Constantine to the present was a grand misstep, a dead-end detour. We will have much more to say about this version of The Rumor. (See chapter 3.)

A Renewal Movement from Within

A final variation of The Rumor holds that the mainline denominations will be reformed from within. Some sociologists and renewal movement adherents are fond of claiming that, given the recalcitrance of institutions including denominations, meaningful change can only come from those who organize within the institution to make their point. Examples we know best from the ELCA are groups such as Word Alone, Lutherans for Life, the Society of the Holy Trinity, and Lutherans Concerned. In a free society and in denominations that use democratic processes, anyone has the opportunity to organize, gather resources, and solicit members, and once organized, attempt to influence denominational policy or practice. At the very least, they provide followers with an arena for support and mutual edification.

While there is truth to the claim that religious groups have been changed by renewal movements from within, it seems an overstatement that this kind of change is *the* wave of the future or that the movements will replace denominations. Instead, it is likely that there will always be people who feel passionately about issues and causes or who get upset with a denomination over some decision, emphasis, or choice of leaders. If the frustration becomes too great, the renewal movements are likely to leave the denomination and start their own, re-creating all the characteristics and functions of the denomination they just left. It is important to remember that over time all organizations begin to look alike. But, the most basic problem with the current wave of renewal movements is their politicalization. As these groups form, they become so preoccupied with clarity about their own identities that they establish boundaries without nuance. It is always "us" versus "them." "Right" versus "wrong." In the process of becoming a group, the group ends up at the extremes of the denomination or at the very least being preoccupied with a very narrow segment or aspect of the denomination. Instead, we want to emphasize the core and let diversity and creativity flourish around it.

Wither The Rumor?

We don't intend to predict the future for these old-line institutions, but we do believe that denominations have already made a significant and invaluable contribution to American life. If they are weak and dying, we believe something important is being lost, and it is a loss that will be felt in all of American society.

It is not our intention to end the discussion on denominations, as if we could. It is not our intention to write a definitive work. We, nevertheless, believe that denominations are worth writing and talking about. Our take on denominations is that their time has not and is not running out. They are caretakers of the historic Christian faith. Each offers a unique gift. Each offers an important and potentially unrecoverable point of view about faith and commitment. There is a need for change. The change we seek honors, or at the very least recognizes, the important contributions of the past while it looks to the future for the new and exciting ways of God. Few other groups in American society other than the mainline denominations have the experience and the potential for looking backward and forward at the same time. We urge our readers to slow down in their acceptance of The Rumor that declares the end of the mainline. If it is true, it will be a bad thing. We intend to show that The Rumor of the death of the mainline has, in Mark Twain's words, been an exaggeration. The Rumor, more than anything else, concedes too much. It gives up and looks for a way to fit into the future rather than working for a future that is truly different. Mainline denominations, at their best, have always been out of step with the history and tradition of "American" religion.

While we prefer the generic *denominations* for the churches we have in mind, because we believe that what we have to say is true for the denominational form of religion in America in general. We use *mainline* because it is more specific and more commonly used to denote the groups we know best. As noted above, mainline implies, in the minds of many, a privileged status from which the mighty have fallen or moved to the sideline. We believe that is an unbalanced view. The competition for the religious hearts of the people of the New World has never been won, at least for long, by any single religious group. The Rumor seems to assume that those most in touch with the popular religious milieu have done and will do better than others. The ebb and flow of religiousness in America is more complex than that assumption and much more interesting. The winner, if there is one, has always been religious individualism, a heartfelt faith. This individualistic approach to the faith has held the stage from the earliest days of the Republic. We don't see that as necessarily good or even inevitable, though it is very powerful.

Finally, our concession to *mainline* makes us worry only about how the label obscures the unique history and set of possibilities inherent in each of the U.S. denominations—a subject for another book. Some came into their own as distinctly American institutions, while others grew by staying close to their European roots. In any case, they are indistinguishable in the minds of most casual observers. Past contributions and the possibilities of the future are missed in a cloud of negative self-fulfilling rumors. But we persist in using *mainline* because we believe the term also represents the best hope of the churches' ability to engage themselves and the culture in a conversation about faith and society that is a real, responsible dialogue. Where else could such a conversation take place? Using the ELCA as a frequent example (because it is the basis of our most direct experience), we will make a case for seeing denominations in a light that is both sympathetic and hopeful, balanced and realistic.

What's Ahead?

In 1942, the German theologian and church leader Dietrich Bonhoeffer prepared an assessment of the monumental struggles of the Confessing Church in Nazi-dominated Germany. Bonhoeffer offered the assessment as a gift to his friends, family, and colleagues for reflection on where they had been and where they might be headed. The title was "After Ten Years." In one sense, it is ludicrous to compare contemporary American mainline denominations to a church fighting for its life and the future of the Christian faith itself in the Germany of Bonhoeffer's time. There are, however, three similarities worth remembering. It has been about ten years since the predictions of denominational decline finally made it to the mass media. Are the mainline denominations losers? Bonhoeffer encouraged his friends not to see the losses they were experiencing as "lost years" but as a chance to learn, reassess, and move forward. Relying on God's grace and guidance, Bonhoeffer also advocated *honesty* in any assessment, including the tough question, "Are we still of any use?" Third, Bonhoeffer's essay boldly claimed that the view from the *margins* of society gave a clearer picture than the one in which the church was a dominant force. "We see . . . from below," he wrote (1991:268). In that spirit, we hope what follows will be useful in approaching denominations as flawed but useful, perhaps more useful and hopeful than sometimes thought, and open to change. Denominations *have* changed over the years. They will continue to change as they wrestle with their identities and their mission.

There are three major sections to this book: Perspectives, Prospects, and Possibilities.

Perspectives
Chapter 1: Conceptual Tools
What are the tools needed to better understand what's going on? In this section we offer our analysis of modernity and post-modernity. Wrestling with the meaning of these two eras will help us to think more clearly. We spend time with the concept of identity, which we believe is

a key to a productive future for the mainline denominations. We also more clearly define what we mean by the mainline. The theology of Dietrich Bonhoeffer will be referenced in the following analysis. We will explain why.

Chapter 2: Fragments of Fragments

How did we come to have denominations? How do they fit in the history of religion in America? In this chapter we set out in detail our view of the place and function of denominations in America. We begin with the disestablishment of religion in America. The First Amendment to the Constitution of the United States forced religious people to find an organizational alternative to the state. The religious leaders needed an organizational means to shape their work and safeguard their religious traditions and heritage in this new free market of religious competition. Denominations emerged as associations of clergy and later took on the broader programmatic work of the national churches. We end the chapter with a description of how several major U.S. denominations are now structured. That structuring did not take place in a vacuum but was the result of negotiation and compromise. Over time, denominations have structured and restructured again as they have evolved into the contemporary organizations they are.

Chapter 3: A Bewildering Course of Events

In the decades since their founding, the fortunes of mainline denominations have ebbed and flowed, but The Rumor takes the 1950s as a major watershed reference point. There was tremendous growth in the membership of denominations in the United States from the late 1950s to 1965. The population was growing dramatically, and amidst this growth the denominations built more elaborate and centralized administrative organizations. By so doing, the mainline denominations believed they were becoming key instruments in the creation of what we call an "American Community." But soon they found themselves on the defensive. The individualistic, popular forms of religion in America reassert themselves again and again.

Prospects

Chapter 4: Numbers

We follow up the commentaries with our view of the most recent numbers. We trace membership figures and financial figures, but we spend most of our time on the question of denominational identity. Do people in the mainline denominations have a distinct identity? What are they telling us through those numbers?

Possibilities

Chapter 5: Built to Last

Experts in the field of organizational theory and practice have found that the *interaction of identity and mission* helps explain why some organizations are successful and competent. That interaction is one key to understanding the possible future of denominations. Do organizations that last exhibit certain strengths? If so, what are they? Do denominations have any of these strengths?

Chapter 6: Incidents of Renewal

In this chapter we review some denominational initiatives that show potential. We describe nine categories of renewal and provide examples.

Chapter 7: Style and Ability: A Way Forward

In this short chapter we draw some conclusions about the incidents of renewal. Five *abilities* and four *styles* of denominations are at work in these examples of renewal. These abilities and styles offer an important guide to the future.

Chapter 8: Toward the Next Rumor: Findings, Worries, Strategies

Here we wrap it all up. What did we find? What worries us? What are the challenges? Are there strategies that might help?

1. CONCEPTUAL TOOLS

For the church to live into its mission, for God's people to be formed in faith, parish and people must reappropriate tradition, honoring it and reforming it at the same time.
   —Diana Butler Bass, 2000

B efore we can go very far with the details, we want to craft a small set of conceptual tools. They will make the job of chasing down The Rumor a bit easier.

Tool 1: A Tale of Two Eras (Modernity and Its Discontent)

Charles Dickens wrote in *A Tale of Two Cities,* "It was the best of times. It was the worst of times." The Rumor is often constructed around concepts that have moved from their academic origins into the less precise world of common parlance. These concepts are used as shorthand for explaining broad cultural trends that impact all of life, including its religious expressions. We hesitate to adopt this shorthand because it is so widely used by so many different people. In the speech of so many, the shorthand ends up meaning different things. It loses its meaning. We do not want to contribute to tossing concepts about without sufficient precision. We hesitate because we know how easy it is to fall into the trap, to do the very thing we call into question. Still, we have to start somewhere.

Modernity

Something is certainly astir. Isn't that always the case? Perhaps we are at the end of an era. But, eras don't just end, they blend into each other. In any case, something new, or more likely something that has always been there, appears to be breaking out of the old, commonly referred to as "modernity." While any attempt to define modernity will come up short, it has to do with processes of "rationalization." Following the sociologist Max Weber, modernity is the era of the extension of the process of rationalization into every aspect of life. Rationalization defines modern life. The processes of rationalization involve a "systematic and unambiguous" orientation toward explicit and fixed goals. Rationalization involves the extension of "the methodical attainment of a definitely given and practical end by means of an increasingly precise calculation of adequate means" (Weber, 1946:293). These processes shape the way modern people think and act.[1] These processes exert their power in social, political, *and* religious institutions. All these institutions begin to act like each other. Over time, they become more and more *like* each other. In modern society the point of all organizations is to efficiently accomplish a goal. Put differently, organizations organize to achieve a purpose(s). Then, they attempt to put in place the means to achieve that purpose. Often this involves, in Weber's word, "calculation." Purpose-setting and calculating to achieve goals are the ways of modernity; a means of bringing "order" out of "chaos."

Rationalization (modernity), however, is a mixed bag. Modernity (rationalization) has created unimagined wealth and a new "middle" class and a tremendous economic cosmos of wealth built on rational or bureaucratic principles. Great masses of people live at previously unthinkable levels of luxury. Education is no longer the exclusive domain of the elite but is now the possession, or within reach, of the masses. Political freedom, unthinkable in traditional societies, is now a reality, or at least a goal, in the world's great modern states based on the rationalized rule of law. But at the same time, modernity ripped through the past, "exposing" whatever it considered irrational (traditional). The old "order," with religion as one of its key props, found itself under attack. The great writers of the modern era as defined by those who determine such things, built their reputations on "exposing" the old, and they started with the "unmasking" of religion. Karl Marx (1978:154) was convinced that the idea of God and other such "superstitions" were "phantoms" of our brains that had taken on "life." Freud (1961:47) was absolutely sure that religious ideas "are not precipitates of experience or end-results of thinking but fulfillments of the oldest, strongest and most urgent wishes of mankind [sic]."[2] Without the old traditions, however, oppressive, new, modern "religions" sprang up—imperialism, fascism, communism, and on and on. Each of these new "religions" claimed science as opposed to tradition or charisma as their source of legitimacy. Science was expected to end the battles. Science was supposed to settle things, but by the end of the twentieth century, each of these rational or scientific "truths" led people to commit unspeakable horrors.

Denominations, ironically, came into being in America as "modern" institutions even while they sought to protect and preserve a "traditional" faith (and its organizational forms) from assault. Like most Americans, religious leaders focused on the work at hand and with the new freedom found success, but not without costs. When old religious forms wrap themselves in rational or bureaucratic principles, contradictions break through. The traditions with the strongest Old World roots were most likely to recognize and feel the weight of these contradictions, and in that way, they were the least "American." Conservative Lutherans, for example, never quite understood how there could be more than one "confessional" church. Everyone claimed "the" truth and engagement meant inevitably exposing one's own claims to the corrosive effect of others. But Lutherans, as if America left much of a choice, embraced the denominational form. They hoped to keep to themselves as much as possible for protection, but by the mid-nineteenth century, they were arguing about what it meant to be "American" Lutherans as opposed to Lutherans in America. There were new American rules. The criteria for making judgments had shifted. Growth mattered. Getting things done mattered. Bishops, for example, might claim religious authority, but in America they were expected to prove themselves by showing considerable administrative skill. Some denominations refused to call their leaders bishops and instead named them presidents as if to say to their religious leaders, "You're elected and you can be un-elected."

Much of the debate about whether America is one of the most secular places on earth, or the most Christian, comes out of the collision of these traditional and modern sensibilities. On the one hand, denominations are compelled to go out and get members. They have proven effective at doing so, especially when held up to the state churches in Europe. On the other hand, the denominations that are most effective at getting members spend much of their time consigning their rivals, close and far, to hell. The "truth" comes down to an effective offensive attack, undermining the truth claims of rivals and gaining a foothold with the masses. Evidence of truthfulness is based on the number of converts, which in the eyes of many traditionalists is the very essence of secularism; the sacred reduced to the profane; to the common, everyday, rational or bureaucratic principles of accounting.

Over the years, now centuries, American denominations have shown remarkable strength and resilience in the face of these contradictions. They have largely preserved their special views of the faith, but they haven't emerged unscathed. Some commentators believe that denominations have become little more than administrative organizations and have lost sight of religion's most basic function—providing a sense of ultimate meaning. We hesitate at both these claims. Some believe that denominations are too bogged down in their traditions to respond adequately to the latest, most popular conception of religious need. Mainline denominations, however, have spent much of their time, perhaps too much, negotiating these powerful contradictions. If they have failed, they should receive high marks for effort. They have asked the important questions: "How do we live in (with) the modern world without falling victim to its corrosive excesses?" "How do we manage the contradictions of form and faith?" "How can we engage the society without losing our own sense of who we are?" The mainline denominations suffer under the weight of the contradictions of modernism, but they have also been able to keep sight of what we call "an American Community." And, it is the search for and working toward a community that is both peaceful and just, with Jesus as our guide, that is one of the most basic functions of Christian religion. Mainline denominations are modern institutions seeking ways to mediate between the old and the new, hoping for the best. Engagement with the world, however reluctant, defines them. They cannot adopt the strategy of expecting everyone to become like them and shouldn't have to. At the same time, they need to know who they are (the essence of their identity) and to make a good case for it. It is a lot to ask.

Post-Modernity

Maybe the day of modern institutions, however, is passed. Continental philosophy has certainly moved on, or at least it likes to think it has. In the last half of the twentieth century, many have argued that we entered a new era. The old "unmaskers" have themselves been "unmasked." And, it is this unmasking of the unmaskers that defines "postmodernity" (if the term has any meaning left in it). Philosopher John Caputo (2001:37) puts it:

Contemporary philosophers have grown increasingly weary with the "old" Enlightenment.[3] Their tendency has been more and more to unmask the modern unmaskers, to criticize the modernist critiques, to grow disenchanted with the disenchanters, to question modernity's prejudice against prejudice, and to look around for a new Enlightenment, one that is enlightened about the (old) Enlightenment. That has inevitably led to a break within their own ranks on the hot topic of religion, where even otherwise "secular" intellectuals have become suspicious of the Enlightenment suspicion of religion.

A new reformation? Well, religion is "back," at least in some quarters. But, post modernity shares a bit with the premodern. Modernity has been passed by (if not through). Anything associated with the old Enlightenment is now under a new suspicion and that includes denominations. Better to be premodern (neo-pagan).[4] It gives a defender of denominations great pause. It is our view that the denominations played a significant role in keeping faith alive by negotiating the contradictions of modernism (making gains and taking losses). But now, because denominations are modern institutions (and they truly are modern institutions), they are neither old enough nor new enough. And, as if the old unmaskers weren't enough, denominations face a new set of disenchanters. Now, the critics are as likely to be "religious" as secular, proclaiming the coming of post-Christendom. The denominations, according to these detractors, have outlived their usefulness since religion is out of "danger" and back in vogue. We cry foul. Denominations can't win for losing. Look out! There is a new set of dangers that look remarkably like the old.

We know that some will think our parameters for understanding what's going on are written too large, but it is important to grasp how modern–postmodern thinking shapes the assumptions. Those promoting a post-Christendom expect a new "apostolic" network to connect individual congregations (or at least a coalition of the willing) to each other for support. This network will be short on regulation and long on independent entrepreneurship in a competitive market where only the most adaptive (the strong) will survive. Our point is that this new Enlightenment is not so postmodern because it has brought a big part of the old (maybe even the most corrosive part of modernity), along for the ride. Congregations with a different *modus operandi* are thought to be in trouble. Some will realize their dire straits and "learn" enough to focus on smaller, niche markets, but those who are truly enlightened will understand the power of the local and meet the needs of individuals who have come out to play in this new, safer "religious" era. Wants and needs will set the new direction as opposed to the traditions of the past. Gather at the feet of the charismatic pastors of the mega churches and learn from the masters who have empirically (there's that modernity again) demonstrated their worth; *or* hold on to the old ways and serve as caretakers for the old-timers until they pass on. A third alternative is needed, and quickly.

We love the fact that it is safe to be religious again, but our patience is short with the heralding of the supposed virtues of a new postmodern era. It keeps the worst of the old modern era, at least as it is described by its proponents. Religious groups are still competing with each other, trying to do each other in. This may be the only way we can live, but it is no sign we have embarked on something new or revolutionary. No, the debate will continue in post-Christendom just as in the old. Claims to the truth will be settled by the numbers. What's so postmodern about that?

Carefully Tweaking Modernity

Buried on the last page of Weber's *The Protestant Ethic and the Spirit of Capitalism* is the line: "The modern man is in general, even with the best will, unable to give religious ideas significance for cultural and national character which they deserve" (Weber, 1958:183). We are not exactly sure what Weber meant as he wrote this sentence, but it appears that modern people have lost the ability to find religion meaningful except in some personalized, individualistic way. If this is true, it makes us shudder. We should all worry about "new" dangers in a postmodern society that takes its religious marching orders from the economic marketplace that starts with the individual first and never quite makes it to the community. In this environment, weak and fading religious traditions are no match for efficient, now supply side, free market, rationalized "churches." The only thing new about postmodernism is its renewed penchant for even weaker religious ties and a shallower spirituality. We don't want to idealize the past, but we don't think this kind of "newness" is either new or a good thing. We can do better!

What's to guide us? Maybe this fear is misplaced or a weak place to hang a defense of denominations, but it is, nevertheless, a way to move toward the future with some of the old traditional past in hand. This may sound reactionary, but it may also be a way forward. The consumer mentality should be reined in a bit. There are good things about modernity that can be used in defense of denominations. We intend to follow John Caputo's (2001:61) lead (speaking from the philosophical heights):

I insist that the post-secular [post-modern] style should arise by way of a certain iteration of the Enlightenment, a continuation of the Enlightenment by another means, the production of a New Enlightenment, one that is enlightened about the limits of the old one. The "post" in the "postsecular" should not be understood to mean "over and done with" but rather after having passed through modernity, so that there is no danger of the emergence of an irrational relativistic left, on the one hand, or of a lapsing back into a conservative pre-modernism masquerading under the guise of postmodern, on the other hand. . . . A more enlightened Enlightenment . . . has a post-critical sense of critique that is critical of the idea that we can establish air-tight borders around neatly discriminated spheres or regions like knowledge, ethics, art and religion. By carefully tweaking modernity, we can give it a post-modern twist.

This book tries to "carefully tweak" mainline denominations and in so doing, give them a twist. If American Christendom is dead, so be it. We should, however, be "careful." In the end, we want the words that Nancy Ammerman (1994b:352) writes about congregations to apply to entire denominations:

They [congregations, but for our purposes denominations] are neither the "lifestyle enclaves" of individualistic religious consumers nor the traditionalistic throwbacks to an earlier time. They are social creations of the modern world, encompassing a both/and quality of modern social life, not an either/or accommodation. They are gatherings of individuals who choose to be there. . . . In this system of choice (and the pluralism it implies), congregations are thoroughly modern institutions. Yet they are communal gatherings, collectivities, that afford their members an opportunity for connection with persons, groups, divine powers, and social structures beyond their own individuality.

Post-Modernity and Organizations

There could be clues to how denominations will fare in a post-modern world or a modern/post-modern mix, by looking at how organizations in general might be affected. William Berquist offers such a view. In his book, *Post-Modern Organization* (1993), Berquist describes the effects of these developments on five aspects of organizational life. The issues have to do with:

- Size and complexity—Can the center hold?
- Mission and boundaries—Who are we?
- Leadership—Who moves us and how?

- Communication—How do we tell our story?
- Capital and worker values—What matters in this organization?

The bottom line is that the post-modern organization will need to be clear about purpose and identity, develop creative ways to build community around identity and purpose, and strengthen ways to handle internal disagreement and conflict while moving together towards a shared future. And, in what seems like a contradiction, boundaries will have to be drawn that are simultaneously porous and inclusive. This challenge for post-modern organizations applies to mainline denominations, but we are getting ahead of ourselves.

Tool 2: Identity and Its Relationship to Mission

Not only do concepts move from academic life to popular usage, they sometimes migrate from one academic discipline to another. Identity is one of those concepts lifted out of its original moorings in the study of personality and put to a different use—the search for understanding organizations. This migration of concepts associated with "persons" (like the apostle Paul in the New Testament referring to the church as "body") to the "collective" side of human behavior isn't always successful, but in the case of denominations (as organizations), it seems helpful to employ the knowledge that surrounds identity as a tool to increase our capacity at finding out what's up with denominations these days. We have pointed out that it is difficult to get people to change their religious habits. Lutherans are not likely to become Southern Baptists (though moving from a Lutheran congregation to an Episcopal congregation isn't too much of a stretch.) In a summary of studies on religious giving, for example, Mark Chaves and Sharon Miller (1999:178) say: "There appears to be no way to make Lutheran or Presbyterian per capita giving rise to the level of Mormon or Seventh-day Adventist giving without making Presbyterian and Lutheran religious traditions into something other than what they currently are." How do we explain this "fixedness" and what does it mean to organizations?

In his classic studies of identity, Erik Erikson observes that identity involves three dynamics: the more durable features of personality over time, an engagement of the issues and the needs of the times, and attempts at self-cure. (See Erikson 1958, 1964, 1969.) All three of these aspects of identity can be used to understand denominations. Denominational histories as well as recent strategic planning exercises usually address not only the question "Who are we?" but "What have we always been?" What elements of "us" have been consistently evident over the years, popping up again and again? The Web site of the United Church of Christ includes a page on "Things We Did First." Without arrogance, but as a statement of fact, the UCC proudly says that they were a bit ahead of everyone else, not followers but leaders. Implication: "You might want to check us out." Being out in front is part of the identity of the UCC.

The UCC Web site list of firsts is also an illustration of Erikson's second dynamic of identity, which is engaging the times. The UCC says, in effect, "We took on more issues. We didn't run away. We may not be perfect but we are courageously operating from within a sense of who we are."

After Erikson, the psychotherapist Rollo May (1969) connected identity with having an effect on the world around us. In a famous passage, May moved identity from a static concept (durable qualities), linking it to the competence motive also developed in the field of psychology.

> The old myths and symbols by which we oriented ourselves are gone, anxiety is rampant; we cling to each other and try to persuade ourselves that what we feel is love; we do not will because we are afraid that if we choose one thing or one person we'll lose the other, and we are too insecure to take that chance. The bottom then drops out of the conjunctive emotions and processes—of which love and will are the foremost examples. The individual is forced to turn inward; he becomes obsessed with the new form of the problem of identity, namely, Even-if-I-know-who-I-am, I-have-no-significance. I am unable to influence others. The next step is apathy. And the step following that is violence. For no human being can stand the perpetually numbing experience of his own powerlessness (May, 1969:13).

Why this excursus into psychology? Because it reinforces the linkage between identity and mission in the study of denominations. Put another way, it is not enough for denominations to have a strong grasp of their identities. There is a lot of that going on. (See chapter 6 for examples of identity formation.) The search for identity must be accompanied by bold attempts to do mission in the world. If it isn't, the cup gets filled but not poured out for the sake of the world. We claim it is in the interplay of identity with mission that denominations will have a future. They go together. It is not enough to know who we are (identity). Likewise, it is not enough simply to do "mission." Identity and mission have to go together, and together they provide a promising path to the future.

Is there any study of identity in the theory and practice of organizations? Yes. Laurence Ackerman (2000), in his book *Identity Is Destiny,* uses his considerable experience as an organizational consultant and leader to illustrate how many of the "fads" (for example, reengineering, total quality management, downsizing) fail, not because of innate flaws, but because of their inappropriate use by organizations. Whenever these practices come up against an organization's identity, the identity survives.

Ackerman cites a 1999 Conference Board report on postmerger integration, that of the factors most instrumental in designing a new effective merged organization, the foremost was attention to basic identity, core values, and strategy. Ackerman believes that present in the dynamics of identity are certain "laws," which if violated, wreak havoc. For our purposes the laws are unimportant. What is important is the relationship of mission to identity. Doing mission effectively is dependent upon a full understanding of the opportunities within (and limits of) identity. It is a little corny but can serve as a memory device to note that "dent," as in making a dent on the world, is in the word itself—i-*dent*-ity. Self-knowledge as a basis for influencing the world presents the best prospect for mainline denominations. Generic solutions to the problems of denominations such as closing seminaries, downsizing national offices, and on and on, presume that these are the pressing issues while we believe identity and its relationship to mission are preeminent. Mainline denominations are what they are and we don't want them to somehow jump out of their collective skins to become something else. We want them to embrace much more fully who they are. Until they do, the quick fixes are no fixes. The tradition must be simultaneously honored and reformed. It must be *re-presented,* that is, brought forward, made present in a useable way from which mission flows.

One of the best examples of how identity interacts with mission to help denominations make ongoing policy decisions is found in a wonderful study of the Amish. Donald Kraybill's (1990) appreciation for Amish religion and social life leads him to an insight which is quite the opposite of the common perception of the Amish—that they don't change their ways of doing things. Of course they change, says Kraybill, but the changes are always worked out in compromise while staying in touch with Amish identity. How does this work?

> The Amish are willing to change, but not at the expense of communal values and ethnic identity. They are willing to use modern technology, but not when it disrupts family and community stability. The cultural compromises, rather than foolish contradictions, are negotiated deals that preserve the integrity of Amish identity while also tapping many of the benefits of modern life. This allows members to enjoy the best of both worlds. This flexibility has enhanced the economic vitality of the

Amish community and also helps them retain their youth. Biological reproduction, cultural resistance and cultural compromise—the three major pieces in the Amish growth puzzle—have enabled them to flourish as a distinctive people in the twentieth century (Kraybill, 1990:11).

We believe this dynamic interplay of identity and mission, who we are and what we do to influence the world, helps explain why denominations are as they are and provides a clue to what they will be and do in the future.

Tool 3: Bonhoeffer

A third conceptual tool comes as encouragement, no, demand, in the thought and writings of Dietrich Bonhoeffer. Bonhoeffer was a Lutheran pastor, university professor, Confessing Church leader, and ecumenical advocate whose letters, books, lectures, fiction, and sermons spark continuing interest and admiration. His participation in a plot to assassinate Adolf Hitler eventually led to his imprisonment and death by hanging on April 9, 1945. He was thirty-nine years old.

To read Bonhoeffer is to be ushered into the world of a person who was simultaneously at home with complex intellectual pursuits and the everyday life of family, music, church, and politics. He once took responsibility for a confirmation class of young boys from a poor neighborhood, throwing out the "curriculum," establishing relationships, and buying them presents at Christmas time. His model for the class was a "worshiping community" in which "pastoral conversion" took place (Bethge, 2000:227). This class can be seen as a precursor of his later work with seminary students as described in his classic book *Life Together* (Bonhoeffer, 1996). Yet his two dissertations (yes, two) on the sociology of the church and the relation of philosophy and ontology to theology established his credentials in the German academy.

Dietrich Bonhoeffer was professor, pastor, and loyal family member. For him, thought, prayer, and action belonged together. One implication for the purpose of this book is to delve deeper beneath slogans and quick judgments to discover paths of responsible action, if and when they present themselves. Bonhoeffer would probably be amused with the facile programmatic recommendations of some of the literature on the mainline's future. To such prescriptions, he might suggest going a bit deeper. Bonhoeffer would, however, be sympathetic with the efforts to reach out beyond ethnic histories and to work with the poor, the "stranger," and those oppressed. This voice from the past speaks across the differences of time and setting in at least three ways pertinent to the themes of this book.

Arrival at a Juncture

Bonhoeffer's world collapsed. Behind his well-known question, "Who is Jesus Christ for us today?" may be another question, "What went wrong?" Everything he valued—friends, family, work, church, and political structure—was taken from him. He kept at it, trying to make "sense" of it, constructing honest and direct probes. As early as 1932–1933, he described a "power" at work that would force an either/or decision, a yes or a no answer. Compromise was not possible. He was dealing with five failures. The hoped-for overthrow of Hitler from within by army generals never came. The "German Christians" caved in, adopting the requirement of "Aryan" for all pastors as barter for privileged treatment from the Hitler regime. The Confessing Church movement of those opposed to Nazism, after early promise and some international ecumenical acceptance, failed in Bonhoeffer's eyes to strongly oppose Hitler's treatment of the Jews and defend its pastors from taking the oath of personal loyalty to Hitler. The ecumenical movement in which Bonhoeffer had labored and to which he looked for understanding and support (with some exceptions) did not seem to "get it" and did not want to. And, most of all, the "normal" standards of ethical actions—reason, principles, conscience, freedom, virtue, duty—failed under the pressure of this "evil disguised as light" (Bonhoeffer, 1991:256–258). Is it any wonder, in prison, he longed for a Christianity not on the boundaries but at the center, or for words whose very utterance would transform lives in freshness and power as did those of Jesus (Bonhoeffer, 1991:297). When one reaches such a juncture—the very decay of religion itself—what does one do? As we chase down The Rumor of decay, decline, and death of the mainline form of Protestantism in America, we are not facing so urgent or dramatic a case as Bonhoeffer did. Even so, decay is decay.

Bonhoeffer helps in at least two important ways. First, he did not lament the loss of power of the Church. Instead, he found assurance in the powerlessness of the Cross. "God lets himself be pushed out of the world on to the Cross. He is weak and powerless in the world and this is precisely the way, the only way, in which he is with us and helps us" (Bonhoeffer, 1991:291). The future of the mainline, following this path, is not in restoration of actual or perceived preeminence as suggested in the term *mainline*. The mainlines need not feel sorry for themselves or long for past glory. Their future lies, to use a Bonhoeffer phrase, in participation in the being of Jesus in the world. Displacement from power is an opportunity to serve. Already we are wandering into themes that address the mainline's plight.

Second, Bonhoeffer's treatment of the "past" is instructive for the mainlines. Like many prisoners before (Paul writing to the Philippians) and since, Bonhoeffer dwelt on the passage of time. One poem, "The Past," is preserved, but his essay, "The Feeling of Time," has been lost except for notes made in its preparation (Green, 2000:2–3). When the present is impoverished and the future is uncertain and uncontrollable, the past becomes preoccupation. We sense this is a temptation for the mainline. Bonhoeffer disagreed with his fiancée, Maria, who felt the past, being past, was of little use. Quite the contrary, he searched the past for memories that would comfort, guide, and inspire. "What else do I have?" he seemed to reason. But here's the catch. The past is a trap. It cannot be restored. It cannot be recaptured or reproduced. As much as Bonhoeffer appreciated the past, he spent most of his prison time imagining what the future hope of Christianity might be, especially one that did not require the hallmarks of religion. In the outline of a book he planned to write but never did (or at least a copy does not remain), the first chapter is titled "A Stock-Taking of Christianity." In his notes on this section, he observed that the Church's primary style was too defensive and was not willing to take risks for others (Bonhoeffer, 1991:274).

Denominations can make two mistakes about the past: trying to bring it back or forgetting it. We see evidence of both. Forgetting the past seems to be the basis for many attempts at reinventing the church. Futures are prescribed for denominations that would have them become something they are not now, never have been, and never will be. The past, as a rich resource to be mined for treasure useful for today and tomorrow, is an implication of Bonhoeffer's thought.

Observations of the Church in the United States

Bonhoeffer visited the United States twice. He spent a postgraduate year at Union Theological Seminary in New York, 1930–1931. The second visit in 1939 was a tortured three weeks evaluating offers to teach and work with his growing realization that coming to the United States was a "mistake" at this time in the life of his beloved nation, Germany. The occasion of this second visit provided a chance to record his observations of denominations in the United States. He titled it "Protestantism without Reformation." We choose only one point from this sometimes scathing, but fair, essay. Bonhoeffer believed that denominations were too grateful to the government for their freedom. The separation of church and state was the church's birthright. The church has the right to expect the state not to interfere. The church with the gospel has the power to make its own room in the world. It is not dependent on the state to grant freedom. The church *has* freedom. In this way, the church will not trade "essential freedom" for institutional freedom (Bonhoeffer, 1991:206).

Bonhoeffer found leaders of churches in America to be so beholden to the government for the church's freedom that they didn't ruffle feathers. The church fought for its privileged role, not for the poor and oppressed. The financial independence of denominations in the United States did not lead, necessarily, to a bold witness in the world or taking risks for others.

The denomination is the unique form created by the separation of church and state. Bonhoeffer sensed that the freedom of denominations was too readily being enjoyed; for example, we worship as we please, rather than using it for strong proclamation and witness.

Person-in-Community

In Bonhoeffer's thought the individual and the community are not linked or joined. They are already one. The primary attribute of American religion is the "heartfelt" (see chapter 2). One either gives in to this reality or attempts to "correct" it, as difficult as that may be. Bonhoeffer is a good guide for "correction." A person is freed from self through God's grace in Christ and is, at the same time, turned to God *and* neighbor. The neighbor, or the "other" as Bonhoeffer sometimes described this dynamic of Christ's work, is not secondary or an afterthought to reconciliation to God. As early as 1932–1933, in his lectures on *Creation and Fall*, Bonhoeffer describes the relation of Adam and Eve as the experience of the "limit" of one to the other (Bonhoeffer, 1997:98–99): "The Other is the limit of my freedom and thereby defines and forms who I am." Later when Bonhoeffer speaks of the Jesus who is there for Others or the Church for Others, he is not mouthing a pious slogan but rather stating the result of Christ's work. He assumes that everyone knows community is where persons meet, and thereby learn who they are (or are not). Writing to a friend about preaching, he suggested a "few simple but vital thoughts. One has to live for some time in a community to understand how Christ is 'formed in it' (Gal. 4:19) and this is especially true of the kind of community that you would have. If I can help in any way, I should be glad to" (Bonhoeffer, 1991:290). The rampant individualism of American Christianity would, in Bonhoeffer's way of seeing things, be a distinct weakness, not a strength. Community building, or better, realizing the God-given nature of the community of faith, would probably be among Bonhoeffer's recommendations for the mainline.

Choosing Dietrich Bonhoeffer for commentary is not intended as a theological veneer on the analysis that follows. Rather, he is but one example (although a good one) of the rich theological resources extant in shedding light on the mainline situation.

Tool 4: Definitions

What do we mean by *mainline?* We know the word is imprecise. Kirk Hadaway and David Roozen (1995:12), for example, decide not to use the word *mainline* because they feel that the term is "imprecise and difficult to define." They go on to note that the same segment of Protestantism is often referred to as "ecumenical, or establishment, or, perhaps most historically accurate, old-line." They (1995:12) prefer the word *mainstream* "because of its emerging popular currency, which makes it a helpful label if properly used in a descriptive, rather than a normative sense." In any case, the "mainstream" includes those religious groups "which in the not too distant past, functioned as an unofficial religious and cultural establishment of the United States, and of Protestantism generally" (Hadaway and Roozen, 1995:13).

We persist in using the term "mainline" simply because we believe more people are familiar with it. We also believe that the general conceptual framework behind the word is widely shared among those who write (and read) about denominations. This framework begins with the acknowledgment that mainline denominations are not presumed to be "better" than other denominations or religious groups, but that these groups have lasted over time and that they have played a significant role in the life of American society and culture. In this sense, these groups are "established." These groups also share "some common theological understandings about the role of the church in society, memberships with somewhat similar socioeconomic characteristics, a sense of historic religious status, and also, increasingly, an awareness that their cultural and religious authority has declined, that as religious bodies they no longer wield the power and influence they once did" (Carroll and Roof, 1993:11).

Wade Clark Roof and William McKinney (1987:6) point out that over the years the word *mainline* has been laid claim to by an increasing variety of groups, not just white Protestants. They note that "many groups—Protestant, Catholic, Jewish, white and nonwhite—that command the loyalties of large numbers of persons and help shape the normative faith and outlook of the population lay claim to being in the mainline." We acknowledge this claim, but it moves us outside the scope of our competence. In terms of specific religious groups, we include in the mainline the Episcopalians, the Presbyterian Church (U.S.A.), the United Church of Christ, the United Methodists, the Disciples of Christ, the American Baptists, the Evangelical Lutheran Church in America, the Lutheran Church–Missouri Synod, the Moravians, and the Reformed Church in America. We do not, however, simply because of the limits of our time and knowledge, give equal time to all these denominations.

2. FRAGMENTS
OF FRAGMENTS

A good history is never just a story but is always an argument, for every history worth its salt is telling us who we are (we who do not know who we are).
—John D. Caputo, 2001

A good history always has a good point. The point of this historical review is to show how the environment for mainline denominations has always been difficult and complex. We believe that mainline denominations have consistently been out of step, despite their mainline moniker, with the dominant religious currents in American society. They have sought to bring a level of order and control to religious beliefs and practices that they have been powerless to affect. Americans are a religious people, but they have always negotiated with organized religion just how they will be religious. In the early republic, only a small portion of the population expressed any commitment to an organized religion, but over time the various faith groups worked hard to increase their membership, and the worshiping population grew.

The total number of congregations expanded from about 2,500 in 1780 to 11,000 in 1820 to 52,000 in 1860 (Butler, 1990: 220). In 2000, there were about 268,000 congregations in the United States with about 141 million members—but that is only part of the story.

It is well established that the framers of the republic were predisposed against any possible centralization of power. They designed the Constitution with its famous checks and balances, and the power of a religious elite was one of their foremost concerns. With the official disestablishment of religion in 1791 through the adoption of the Bill of Rights, including the First Amendment, religious leaders were forced to accept a lesser role. Religious leaders found themselves having to compete for the hearts and minds of a populace that was set free to choose their religious beliefs and practices as they pleased. Individualistic and evangelical forms of Protestantism took the stage in the 1730s, and as the number of converts grew, "personal" religion became America's religion. Religious people in the New World longed for a heartfelt faith, and they found it in the midst of popular revivals (Noll, 2002a). Being religious, as part of a tradition, as part of an organized religious community, was antiquated and Old World. *Organized* religion in America, then as now, was the realm—and the problem—of religious leaders. For the vast majority of regular people, faith in God was a simple and solitary matter of the heart.

Many religious leaders, in spite of disestablishment, tended to see matters differently. Many felt the heartfelt was downright dangerous. Left to its own devices, where would it lead? People without theological training were declaring themselves theologians, interpreters of the faith no longer in need of guidance, much less the proscriptions of an organized church. Organized religion, in popular opinion, cared more about its catechisms, creeds, and confessions than it did about the heartfelt. With the Bible and the guidance of the Spirit, the religious layperson could come to his or her own true knowledge of the faith. A community, to guide and shape belief, was at best a hindrance and at worst a lie. Where there once stood "the church" now stood solitary individuals with their solitary truths and a process that turned fragments (denominations) into fragments. Gordon Wood, historian, writes (1993:332):

> Not only were the traditional Old World churches fragmented but the fragments themselves shattered in what seemed at times to be an endless process of fission. There were not just Presbyterians, but Old and New School Presbyterians, Cumberland Presbyterians, Springfield Presbyterians, Reformed Presbyterians, and Associated Presbyterians; not just Baptists, but General Baptists, Regular Baptists, Free Will Baptists,

Separate Baptists, Dutch River Baptists, Permanent Baptists, and Two-See-in-the-Spirit Baptists. Some individuals cut their ties completely with the Old World churches and gathered around a dynamic leader like Barton Stone or Thomas Campbell. Other seekers ended up forming churches out of single congregations, and still others simply listened in the fields to wandering preachers like the Methodist Lorenzo Dow.

To conservative religious leaders, like the Lutheran Charles Porterfield Krauth, the fragmented religious landscape was cluttered with debris. Faiths of long-standing tradition and substance were reduced to, and drowned out in, endless debate. Krauth (1972:103) was forthright in his views of religion in America:

The denominations around us cover nearly every leading form of Christianity and of its distortions and a number of its smallest bodies, parasites, and parasites of parasites. . . . If our land were searched through all its borders, the number of groups would be seen to be simply appalling—some in vigorous life, some rising, some dying out, some dead and dusty but not swept out of sight, some fossilized into a sort of stony existence, others like soap bubbles expanding in glittering swiftness toward their bursting.

At another point he (1972:48) noted:

We are surrounded by the children of those churches that claim an origin in the Reformation. We sincerely respect and love them; we fervently pray that they may increase in every labor of love. . . . But how shall we make ourselves worthy of their respect and lift ourselves out of the sphere of that pitiful little sectarianism which is crawling over us and biting us continually.

The political elite, many of whom supported disestablishment, had become equally concerned at these developments. Many hoped that the church would fill the gap in the social order left by the wholesale dismantling of government. But once the disestablishment door had been thrown open, organized religion itself was teetering. With the looming prospect of chaos, "the clergy had been repeatedly told that, whatever your doctrinal differences, 'you are all united in inculcating the necessity of morals,' and 'from the success or failure of your exertions in the cause of virtue, we anticipated the freedom or slavery of our country'" (Wood, 1993:334). No matter what their differences, the clergy were called upon to instill moral virtue in the people. Organized religion, no matter what differences separate the groups, promotes this message of goodness to the present day.

Going it Alone, Together

For those with a heartfelt faith, there was freedom in going it alone, but for those who made religion their profession, an organized community with a tradition that honored the past and shaped the future was critical. The ability to sustain religious work over time was dependent upon the power, authority, and legitimacy of organized churches. Even the most independent religious entrepreneurs found organizing religious work a benefit.

> Lorenzo Dow, the itinerant, all but ritualized his cant regarding the evil in the Methodist's hierarchical church government, he denounced Methodist and papal government in nearly every public appearance, and he praised schisms, however wrenching, because they demonstrated that the search for religious truth was still going on. Yet Dow also knew the value and pleasure of authority. In the 1790s and early 1800s he sought and obtained Methodist approbation of his preaching, and even though he formally left the denomination he never eschewed the benefits of its organization. He traveled Methodist circuits throughout his lifetime, and Methodist listeners and local ministers found nothing objectionable in his free-grace theology and in his helpful, perhaps heartfelt, evocation of the original Methodist itinerants (Butler, 1990:287).

The clergy formed professional associations that, in turn, became the basis of the American denominational form. The form was rational—and bureaucratic—from its beginning. Religious professionals gathered together to protect their interests and to bring order and legitimacy to their work. To do so they relied upon Methodist bishops, Presbyterian presbyteries, Lutheran synods, Baptist associations, and Episcopal dioceses.

> They [the leaders] kept schedules, visited congregations in a certain order; inspected church discipline, determined who might or might not receive a "settled" minister, and answered to their superiors when they failed. Together, this planning and labor established lines of spiritual and denominational authority. Itinerants transformed wilderness into frontier and frontier into settlement by tying congregation to

congregation, then melding these into regional and national denominational networks (Butler, 1990:277).

In short, the denominational form of religion in America was a product of the needs and concerns of religious *leaders* who were among the first to apply the rational, bureaucratic forms to their work in America. While some denominations remained largely congregational, independent, or free-church, others developed variations of the extensive rational-bureaucratic structures they had known in Europe. These structures stood in stark contrast to popular expressions of the faith. If denominational organizations were to stand the test of time, they would have to prove their worth. And they would have to do so by a different logic than popular religion. A personal faith could go where it willed—or so it seemed—but denominations were expected to follow a straighter line by effectively and efficiently providing competent pastors for local congregations, then in supporting clergy in their dealings with those same congregations.

The Goals
Setting the Standards and Teaching the Faith
First and foremost, denominations were about ordering the lives of religious professionals. But it was also through *administration,* in particular, setting the standards for religious professionals, that religious leaders found a way to preserve and extend their specific view of the Christian faith in the presence of the heartfelt. Inevitably, the standards for clergy had to do with belief and right behavior, and through the monitoring of the beliefs and behaviors of clergy, denominations found a way to teach the faith in its "correct form" to the regular members of their congregations. John Wesley's "Articles of Agreement" in 1769 committed Methodist preachers to devote themselves entirely to God; to preach the old Methodist doctrines and no others; and to observe and enforce the whole Methodist discipline. Those disciplines were designed to protect Methodism (Heitzenrater, 1997:29). Likewise, Herman Amberg Preus (1990:40) was intent on protecting Lutheranism in the late 1800s when he argued that the primary reason for gathering congregations into synods was "to strengthen the orthodox faith, to preserve unity in a pure confession with respect both to defend against false teachers and to protect against separatism and sectarianism." All this doctrinal ambition for unity and the control of false teaching was mediated and negotiated and often distant from the concerns of regular people. Let the clergy debate standards for ordination. Let the bishops of synods or the presidents of sessions figure out how to organize religion. The people in the

pews wanted a pastor who could stir them deeply and be there in times of need. The clergy wanted a way into the ministry and a way of maintaining their careers over time.

Doing the Work Efficiently

As denominations moved through the nineteenth and twentieth centuries, they took on a second role—the *agency* role. The extent to which denominations began to act as agencies varied from one religious group to the next, but the motivation for making agency work the denomination's work had as much to do with order and efficiency as it did with providing pastors for congregations. Rational principles of administration were applied. In some denominations there was a gathering of independent, voluntary, mission societies. In others, those mission activities were always a more integrated part of the denomination's work.[1] When there is a debate about the agency role of denominations in America, it is usually around the issue of efficiency and how best to achieve it. At one end of the spectrum were those who argued that too much centralization is inefficient because it restrains competition and limits the initiative of religious entrepreneurs. On the other end of the spectrum were those who believed that without centralization there was too little coordination. This led to inefficiency, because too many similar agencies worked to achieve the same goals as they competed for the same scarce resources.[2] Religious leaders like the Lutheran Preus were expert at making the case for centralization based on the value of efficiency. He (1990:40) argued:

> It is our duty to extend the gospel of the kingdom of God as far as possible by all means available for its promotion. Individually the congregations, especially the small ones, can accomplish nothing or next to nothing toward this goal in comparison to what, with blessing, they can accomplish by *joining forces* [our emphasis] and collaborating in the establishment of schools; in the publishing of Bibles, hymnals, confessional writings, school books, and devotional books; and in home and foreign missionary endeavors.

Over time, those favoring centralization gained the advantage.

By the 1920s American denominations of all polities were consolidating their missions, publishing enterprises, and other ventures under one organizational roof. Soon they could draw charts showing the relationship of each part to the whole. Budgets were centralized, and fund-raising was turned over to professionals. . . . Gradually, the people who worked for these organizations were expected to have specific educational credentials, and everyone had a job description. They worked out long-range plans and proposed integrated programs of study. And they began to keep records (Ammerman, 1994a:116).

For the United Methodists, the consolidation began as early as 1872 and was extended in 1939 and in 1968 (Richey, 1997:15). For the Christian Church (Disciples of Christ), a "unified agency structure" was created in 1920 and again in 1968 when the Disciples adopted a "convention/agency" structure (Burkhart, 1980:55). Among the American Baptist Churches, U.S.A., centralization moved slowly through the early years of the twentieth century, and in 1972 the agencies of the church were brought under the umbrella of the convention (Burkhart, 1980:57). Among Lutherans, there were a series of consolidations of different denominational groups that were largely divided along ethnic lines. The United Lutheran Church in America (ULCA) was formed in 1918, bringing together a host of smaller Lutheran groups. That process continued as the ULCA was joined by other Lutherans to form the Lutheran Church in America in 1962. Two years earlier, the American Lutheran Church was formed, also the product of a merger. Finally, in 1988 the Evangelical Lutheran Church in America was organized in the merger of the Lutheran Church in America, the American Lutheran Church, and the Association of Evangelical Lutheran Churches.

The regulatory function of denominations has sometimes been defined apart from the agency function. There is good reason for doing so, since the two functions sometimes appear to be in conflict (Wright, 1984; Chaves, 1993). But the two functions, the certification of clergy and the gathering together of various mission agencies for the sake of efficiency, are both grounded in the processes of rationalization. (See "Conceptual Tools," chapter 1, for a fuller description of this process.)

Organization Building among the Mainlines
Despite the rationale of efficiency, the building of organizations by denominations beyond the local congregation in America has largely been, in practice, an incoherent and haphazard process. We believe this is due to a love-hate relationship with *all* institutions in America, which is intensified in religious settings. On the one hand, the primary movement of religion in America has been the search for, and the satisfaction of, a heartfelt faith. Americans have never been comfortable with the idea of the church as an organization (which can be said of government as well). An anti-institutional bias goes to the core of American religious expression.[3] On the other

hand, Americans love efficiency. Efficiency is always better, and that bit of American mythology dates at least as far back as Benjamin Franklin's *Poor Richard's Almanac.*[4] But, efficiency of any scale is often the result of the application of rational-bureaucratic organizational principles. There is no doubt that the rational-bureaucratic form can also be inefficient, but a mass, democratic society could not exist without bureaucracies. Religious and nonreligious Americans have trouble coming to grips with this dilemma. What does a heartfelt faith have to do with a rational-bureaucratic organization? A well-used strategy is to simply pretend that the church is *not* an organization. A popular phrase used by church leaders is, "The church is an organism, not an organization." Instead of giving careful attention to how the church works or doesn't as an organization, the organization of the church is seldom given its proper due.

Rather than too much centralization and integration, there is far too little in American denominationalism. Rather than too much emphasis on structure, there is far too little. Rather than using structures to facilitate accountability, structures are often used in American denominations to undermine and thwart accountability. Each denomination holds certain theological principles dear, but care for those principles, when it comes to building a structure, most often works itself out in regressive rather than progressive ways. In other words, mainline denominations, from a theological point of view, often know much more clearly what they don't want to do, as opposed to what they do want to do, with regard to structure. These theological principles, however, also tend to be wrapped in American, antiorganizational biases that reflect the ongoing influence and priority of a heartfelt faith. Building an organizational structure is an afterthought, even as it remains necessary. Then, because of this regressive approach to structure, things go wrong, or at least they are more likely to go wrong. The structure, never given its due, turns out to be inadequate, and that opens the door wide for further critique and a host of self-fulfilling prophecies.

Clergy Administration

In the early days of denominations, controls governing clergy, and access to the status of clergy, were the primary work of denominational leaders. The administration of those controls was a relatively straightforward process, because the structure for managing the work could be carried out locally. The annual national conference was an adequate means for establishing the criteria. Local committees could be formed to do the administration, because it was direct and, most importantly, episodic. A bishop or some other church professional could pull it all together using volunteers.

The administrative team could come together, do their work, and go home to their "real" work until they were needed again. But when denominations began to take on the responsibility of agencies that were permanently organized and needed permanent oversight, more structure was needed. To complicate matters further, much of the discussion of structure took place amidst plans for merger between or among two or more already existing denominations with their existing complement of agencies. Structure building didn't start with a blank slate—it never does—but in a highly charged atmosphere of compromise.

Pressure for Unity

Through the middle of the twentieth century, the national expression of many denominations consisted of a "general" meeting alongside a host of loosely related religious agencies. Most of the agencies were formed in the nineteenth century and were not under the direct control of denominational officials. In the last quarter of the nineteenth century there was a push to bring these agencies under more direct influence of the denominations. But the actions to do so were modest. Usually the denominations simply acted to ensure the representation of denominational persons on the board of an agency, with the condition that the agency report to the general meeting. Over time, because it was convenient and more efficient, many denominational agencies began to share infrastructure such as office space.

These circumstances, however, became considerably more complex after the turn of the twentieth century because of the prevalence of denominational mergers. Everyone was talking and many were acting. H. Paul Douglass's (1937) inventory of the period between 1927 and 1936 reports the extent of the activity. The Protestant Episcopal Church was in active conversation with the Augustana Synod (Swedish) Lutheran Church, as well as the Methodist Episcopal Church and the Presbyterian Church, U.S.A. The Baptists of the Northern Convention were talking with the Disciples of Christ. The Evangelical Church was negotiating for union with the United Brethren in Christ. The Reformed Church in the United States merged with the United Brethren in Christ. The Lutheran Synod of Buffalo, the Evangelical Lutheran Synod of Iowa and other states, and the Evangelical Lutheran Joint Synod of Ohio and other states merged to form the American Lutheran Church. The United Lutheran Church in America, the American Lutheran Church, and the Missouri Synod appointed commissions for a joint conference looking toward union. The Methodist Episcopal Church and the Methodist Episcopal Church–South, failed to unite in 1925, but negotiations for union including the Methodist

Protestant Church were immediately renewed. Conversations among representatives of the Methodist Episcopal, Protestant Episcopal, and Presbyterian Church, U.S.A. took place but broke down. The African Methodist Episcopal and the African Methodist Episcopal Zion Churches attempted but failed to affect corporate union. In summary, Douglass notes that three churches mutually recognized each other during this period, thirteen achieved some level of corporate unity, and five moved into federation.

This level of conversation and merger activity demanded conversation about structure. In the minds of many there were too many denominations and too many independent agencies associated with the denominations. What could be done about it? Different denominations employed different strategies, but the primary approach was to merge the work of many similar agencies into one. Then the denominations designed and adopted a unified means for governance and administration. Often, however, finding the means for unified governance and administration was difficult, and the final result was inevitably the product of compromise and negotiation. The values of autonomy and efficiency square off and both take their losses. Illustrations are provided for the United Church of Christ, the United Methodist Church, the Episcopal Church, the Evangelical Lutheran Church in America, and the Presbyterian Church (U.S.A.).

The United Church of Christ
Members: 1.4 million
The circumstances of the United Church of Christ (UCC) illustrate the complexities—perhaps in the most extreme form—of the agency problem. Formed in 1957 by the union of the Evangelical and Reformed Church and The General Council of the Congregational Christian Churches of the United States, the UCC found itself faced with the work of a myriad of agencies. The following section from the UCC's current constitution traces the organizational and administrative history. We quote the constitution at length because the UCC is one of the best examples of how contemporary mainlines have found creative solutions to coordinating previously independent entities as the tensions between efficiency and autonomy are played out, under the umbrella of denominational identity and the desire to do effective mission in the world. Prior agencies are named, one after another, but the work of these agencies—their only "agent"—is one of six "ministry" units of the contemporary UCC.

The Covenanted Ministries . . . acting as successors to and agents for all predecessor bodies related to the United Church of Christ, continue the work, mandates, and legacies previously carried on by the Secretary, Director of Finance and Treasurer, American Board of Commissioners for Foreign Missions, the Board of International Missions, the Commission on World Service, the Congregational Christian Service Committee, the United Church Board for World Ministries, Board of National Missions, Board of Christian Education and Publication, Board of Business Management, Board of Home Missions of the Reformed Church in the U.S., the American Missionary Association, Congregational Church Building Society, Congregational Education Society, Congregational Home Missionary Society, Congregational Publishing Society, The Congregational Sunday School Extension Society, the Congregational Women's Home Missionary Federation, the United Church Board for Homeland Ministries, Coordinating Center for Women in Church and Society, Commission for Racial Justice, Office for Church Life and Leadership, Office for Church in Society, Stewardship Council, Commission on Development, and Office of Communication.

The Office of General Ministries continues the work of, and acts as the agent for, the following predecessor offices or bodies: The President, the Secretary, and the Director of Finance and Treasurer of the United Church of Christ; the Commission on Development; the Stewardship Council; and the Office of Communication. It also continues the following ministries: ministries of research formerly conducted by the United Church Board for Homeland Ministries.

Local Church Ministries continues the work of, and acts as agent for, the following predecessor bodies: the Office for Church Life and Leadership, the Coordinating Center for Women in Church and Society, the Stewardship Council, the United Church Board for Homeland Ministries, and its predecessor bodies: The Board of National Missions, Board of Christian Education and Publication, Board of Business Management, Board of Home Missions of the Reformed Church in the U.S., the American Missionary Association, Congregational Church Building Society, Congregational Education Society, Congregational Home Mission Society, Congregational Publishing Society, The Congregational Sunday School Extension Society, the Congregational Women's Home Missionary Federation.

Justice and Witness Ministries continues the work of, and acts as agent for, the following predecessor bodies: the Office for Church in Society, the Commission for Racial Justice, the Coordinating Center for Women in Church and Society. It also continues the following ministries: ministries of public policy advocacy in the area of communications formerly conducted by the Office of Communication, ministries of prophetic service and action formerly conducted by the Division of the American Missionary Association of the United Church Board for Homeland Ministries, ministries of global advocacy in the U.S.A. formerly conducted by the United Church Board for World Ministries.

Wider Church Ministries continues the work of, and acts as agent for, the following predecessor bodies: the United Church Board for World Ministries, the American Board of Commissioners for Foreign Missions, the Board of International Missions, the Commission on World Service, and the Congregational Christian Service Committee. It also continues the following ministries: ministries of volunteer services formerly conducted by the Division of the American Missionary Association of the United Church Board for Homeland Ministries; ministries of the Health and Welfare Coordinating Council formerly related to the United Church Board for Homeland Ministries. (*Constitution of the United Church of Christ,* 2001. Paragraphs 63–67.)

The highest legislative body of the United Church of Christ is the General Synod, but its power is limited. The UCC has no intention of changing its stripes. "No power vested in the General Synod shall invade the autonomy of Conferences, Associations, and Local Churches, or impair their right to acquire, own, manage, and dispose of property and funds" (*Constitution of the United Church of Christ,* 2001. Paragraph 54). Delegates are chosen at the local Conference level. The General Synod, through its Executive Council and affiliated agencies, is to carry on the work and find support for the work. It has the right to establish and maintain a "national headquarters" and a treasury, to create "bodies" for carrying out its work, and to manage ecumenical relationships. With regard to agencies

the General Synod and its Executive Council shall consider the work of all Covenanted, Affiliated, and Associated Ministries. It shall also correlate their work, publicity and promotion, preventing duplication and affecting economies of administration, so as to secure maximum effectiveness and efficiency through careful stewardship of personnel and financial resources. Due protection shall be given to all trust funds, including pension funds (*Constitution of the United Church of Christ, 2001.* Paragraph 56).

In practice, that correlating, preventing duplication, and achieving economies, effectiveness, and efficiency is no small order. One mechanism for doing so is the "Collegium of Officers," which includes the General Minister (President), the Associate General Minister (both in the Office of the General Ministries), the Executive Minister for Local Church Ministries (Office of Local Church Ministries), the Executive Minister for Wider Church Ministries (Office of Wider Church Ministries), the Executive Minister for Justice and Witness Ministries (Office of Justice and Witness Ministries), and other officers as they may be determined by the General Synod. The Collegium of Officers is a "meeting as peers." It is responsible for providing leadership for the mission programming of the UCC and for the implementation of General Synod actions. "The Collegium provides a setting for mutual accountability, for mutual reporting, and for assessing the ongoing programs of the United Church of Christ." No one controls the Collegium, as the name implies, and each of the Ministries "may retain or secure its own charter and adopt its own bylaws and other rules which it deems essential to its own welfare and not inconsistent with this Constitution and the Bylaws of the United Church of Christ and in accordance with advice and counsel given from time to time by the General Synod" (*Constitution of the United Church of Christ,* 2001. Paragraph 18). The Ministers are elected by the separate boards of their separately incorporated agencies. Each Ministry retains the right to "organize itself as it deems necessary to carry out its program and fulfill its mandates; to determine its budget; and to adopt its own charter, bylaws, and rules of procedure which it deems essential to its own welfare, not inconsistent with the Constitution and the Bylaws of the United Church of Christ" (*Constitution of the United Church of Christ,* 2001. Paragraph 58).

The Constitution goes on to state that "dissolution of the Covenanted Ministry shall occur only with the consent of its Board of Directors, after advice and consultation with the General Synod, and only with provision for the transfer of the ownership, management, and control of its assets and funds to a successor corporation that is legally obligated and empowered to own and carry out the obligations, terms, conditions, and requirements of said assets and funds, as the Board of Directors shall determine" (*Constitution of the United Church of Christ,* 2001. Paragraph 60).

If there is any award for pulling things together in the face of a considerable history of keeping things apart, the UCC richly deserves to receive it!

The United Methodist Church
Members: 8.3 million
One might expect that issues of control would be most extreme in denominations with long congregationalist histories and less a matter for

denominations in the Episcopal tradition, but remarkable similarities exist. The Methodist Church was formed in 1939 in the merger of the Methodist Episcopal Church, the Methodist Episcopal Church–South, and the Methodist Protestant Church (Burkhart, 1980:65). Each of those churches had, at the end of the nineteenth century, brought the governing bodies of their various agencies under the auspices of their respective conventions. At the time of the merger there were similar agencies with similar purposes. "This led to an amalgamation of agencies, but by the 1950s, a need for greater coordination and restructuring of the entire agency system was expressed" (Burkhart, 1980:65). Attempts were made to deal with the problem in 1952, but most of the recommendations of a study commission on structure were not adopted (Tuell, 1997:130). As a result, a diagram of the national expression of the church looked like a circle around the General Convention with each of the agencies essentially reporting directly to the General Convention. Bishop Jack Tuell, retired Methodist bishop, writes (1997:130):

> Power and authority are widely dispersed within the United Methodist Church, undoubtedly deliberately so. We have inherited from the founders of America a rather keen distrust of too much power centralized in one person. There is not only not a head person, there are no headquarters of our Church! This is not necessarily bad, but we should recognize that this general lack of central direction over the years has resulted in our various boards and agencies pretty much going their own independent ways, each developing its own programs, which sometimes have overlapped with programs of our other agencies and sometimes actually conflicted with them. The end result is a situation where our total resources are not always put to the best use, and where passing the buck becomes inordinately easy to do.

In 1968, when the Methodist Church merged with the Evangelical United Brethren Church to create the United Methodist Church, the case for restructuring again moved to the fore. But instead of taking steps to create a more integrated national organization, the General Convention decided in 1972 to add two more agencies, the General Council on Ministries and the General Council on Finance and Administration. While some argued for reducing the number of boards and agencies, another amalgamation was created. The approach to "overlapping and multiple approaches to the annual conferences and the local churches" was to create a General Council on Ministries, while budgetary control was given to *another* newly created agency, the General Council on

Finance and Administration. Even if the creation of these agencies was a step in the right direction, the General Conference didn't go very far. The General Council on Ministries was given a task with limited abilities to perform. The General Council still has no budgetary control, a significant source of power. The General Council on Ministries was also given the responsibility of evaluation, but it has neither the money nor the staff to do the job. No one realistically expects the Council on Ministries to do its assigned task.

In 2000 the General Conference rejected yet another restructuring proposal. This proposal would have dramatically changed the church's structure. Instead, that assembly mandated that the General Council on Ministries "determine the most effective design for the work of the general agencies and . . . provide enabling legislation to the 2004 General Conference." But the proposal presented to the 2004 General Conference for creating a central governance unit called the "Connectional Table" was also rejected. The plan that was adopted calls for a scaled back Connectional Table with modest powers. The separate charters and incorporations of the various church agencies are left intact.

The Episcopal Church

Members: 2.3 million

When it comes to the national structure, The Episcopal Church is only somewhat more integrated than the United Methodist Church. Power and authority remain widely disbursed. The General Convention is the highest legislative body. It consists of the House of Deputies (priests, deacons, and lay people) and the House of Bishops. The General Convention establishes and gives responsibilities to a series of Standing Commissions that have significant responsibility and are required to report to the General Convention. They are funded from the Joint Standing Committee on Program, Budget, and Finance. The Standing Commissions include: Anglican and International Peace with Justice Concerns; Small Congregations; Constitution and Canons; Domestic Mission and Evangelism; Ecumenical Relations; Liturgy and Music; Ministry Development; National Concerns; Stewardship and Development; the Structure of the Church; and World Mission.

In addition to the Standing Commissions there is an Executive Council charged with carrying out "the program and policies adopted by the General Convention." "The Executive Council shall have charge of the coordination, development, and implementation of the ministry and mission of the Church" (Canon 4: Section 1(a)). The national program ministries include the Office for Anglican and Global Relations; Ethnic Congregation Development; Congregational Development; Episcopal Migration Ministries; Peace and Justice Ministries; Ministries with Young People; and Episcopal Relief and Development. The Executive Officer "shall also coordinate the work of the Committees, Commissions, Boards and Agencies funded by the General Convention Expense Budget" (Canon 1: Section 13).

In addition to the national program units, there is the Office of the Presiding Bishop. Under the Presiding Bishop are other offices that primarily focus on the clergy of the church. There is the Church Development Office (which provides support to lay and clergy professionals); the Office for Ministry Development (responsible for theological education, recruitment, training, and deployment of the professionals); the Office of Pastoral Development (which works with the bishops); the Office for Liturgy and Music (which works with the bishop on liturgical matters); and the Office for Ecumenical and Interfaith Relations. While the constitution of the United Church of Christ is careful not to impinge on the rights of congregations, Title 1 of the Episcopal Church leaves the door open for the synods.

> The Synod of a Province may take over from the Executive Council, with its consent, and during its pleasure, the administration of any given work within the Province. If the Province shall provide the funds for such work, the constituent Dioceses then members of, and supporting, such Province shall receive proportional credit therefore upon the quotas assigned to them for the support of the Program of the Church, provided that the total amount of such credits shall not exceed the sum appropriated in the budget of the Executive Council for the maintenance of the work so taken over (Canon 9: Section 9).

The presiding bishop is "charged with responsibility for leadership in initiating and developing the policy and strategy in the Church and speaking for the Church as to the policies, strategies and programs authorized by the General Convention" (Canon 1: Section 4(a)).

The Evangelical Lutheran Church in America
Members: 5.1 million
The Evangelical Lutheran Church in America is the result of a 1988 merger of the American Lutheran Church, the Lutheran Church in America, and the Association of Evangelical Lutheran Churches.

Structurally, this denomination is highly integrated. The highest legislative authority is the Churchwide Assembly. The Churchwide Assembly elects a Church (churchwide) Council. The Church Council is responsible for the overall program of the national offices. The Council does this in conjunction with the presiding bishop and the Cabinet of Executives, which includes the executive directors of the churchwide "units." These units include the Divisions for Congregational Ministries, Higher Education and Schools, Ministry, Outreach, Church in Society, and Global Mission. There are also two commissions, the Commission for Women and the Commission for Multicultural Ministries.

The Office of the Bishop includes departments to assist the bishop with the work of the denomination. These departments include the Departments for Ecumenical Affairs, Synodical Relations, Human Resources, Communication, and Research and Evaluation. The Office of the Bishop controls the budget of the program units working with the Office of the Treasurer. At the same time, the divisions and the commissions have their own governing boards that are elected by the Churchwide Assembly. As a result, each division and commission is semiautonomous within an overall framework of policy and coordination. This coordination also is exercised through the executive directors on a Churchwide Cabinet and through the budgetary control of the Office of the Bishop. At this point, however, a proposal is being made to centralize the governance structure and to create a new set of more integrated programmatic units.

The Presbyterian Church (U.S.A.)
Members: 2.5 million
The Presbyterian Church (U.S.A.) is the result of a merger in 1983 between the Presbyterian Church in the United States and the United Presbyterian Church in the United States. The General Assembly, which has the highest legislative authority, has taken several actions over the years aimed at restructuring its national offices. Administratively, the Presbyterian Church (U.S.A.) has a closely integrated national system.

The General Assembly has a stated clerk who is responsible to the Office of the General Assembly. The stated clerk is responsible for the ecumenical affairs of the General Assembly, and also for the Department for History. Also under the General Assembly is the General Assembly Council. Its primary purpose "is to lead and coordinate the total mission program" of the denomination. The General Assembly Council is staffed by an executive director who is responsible for carrying out the wishes of the General Assembly Council. The members of the General Assembly

Council also sit as boards of the various ministries that carry out the actual programmatic work of the church. There are three ministries, including the Congregational Ministries Division (Christian education and leadership development); the National Ministries Division (evangelism, church development, higher education, racial ethnic ministries, social justice ministries, women ministries); and the Worldwide Ministries Division (global service and witness). Clifton Kirkpatrick, stated clerk of the Presbyterian Church (U.S.A.), has voiced his concern that the challenge facing his church is not so much structural as constitutional. "There is no group of Christian people for whom constitutions are more important than for Presbyterians (Kirkpatrick, 2002:1). That importance may be getting in the way. "We are headed for a 'train wreck' with our regulatory model of the *Book of Order*. We need to be about formulating a new polity for a new century" (Kirkpatrick, 2002:8). This new polity would recover the historic purpose of polity, namely, "to make possible the missionary outreach of the church in its particular culture" (Kirkpatrick, 2002:9).

The Underlying Dynamics

The organization building of the mainline denominations is clearly influenced by a series of important factors. First and foremost, we believe the pattern is governed by the anti-institutional, individualistic tendencies in American culture in general and in American religion in particular. This powerful force, built into the very being of denominations, led to independent agency building. Until the twentieth century, denominations were largely clergy associations, with the program of the denominations being carried out by the independent agencies. The pattern of using independent agencies for the work of the denominations was as developed in the United Methodist Church, with its Episcopal structure, as it was in the United Church of Christ, with its congregational polity. The combination of individualistic tendencies, anti-institutional biases, and the use of autonomous agencies for the work of denominations led to incoherent and haphazard organization building. The people who run national denominations are not directly responsible for this state of affairs—and even many of them may share a preference for a heartfelt faith and an anti-institutional bias. Systems of administration and control are often not in place. Instead, power and authority are widely dispersed. Everyone has a voice, but no one is in charge. As Tuell (1997:130) so clearly put it: "The end result is a situation where our total resources are not always put to the best use, and where passing the buck becomes inordinately easy to do."

Based on this underlying dynamic, the building of the organizational church becomes a political matter. More specifically, it becomes a matter of what Joseph Gusfield (1963) called "status politics," convincing others that a particular value is *the* value and that the church should do something to support and maintain it. Then, people organize politically to get it done. The specific details of how it will get done are left to denominational professionals to figure out, and often they have access to limited resources. "The church should start a hundred new congregations a year," or "the church should build up its campus ministry program," or "the church should underwrite the costs of theological education or subsidize churches in rural areas or the inner-cities." These are the right things to do, and any group of local church people can create a list of these things that goes on for pages. But *organizing* to do these things and *paying to get them done* is seen as someone else's problem—a someone else who works in a system that operates under considerable constraints.

Over time, the national expressions of the denominations have become an amalgamation of program units. Program A runs into Program B, and Program C runs into Programs D and E. Sooner or later, someone or some group asks why the wider church is so disorganized. They see—and point out publicly—inefficiencies and waste. But even the word *efficient* brings baggage with it. Some will ask, "What does the church have to do with efficiency? People need to hear and feel the love of Christ no matter what the costs." The best arguments for efficiency, however, turn into support for good stewardship and those who believe in good stewardship persist. They too go to the General Assembly and call for a committee or commission on structure. The committees meet, issue their findings and proposals, and then, most often, go out of existence. If resources are plentiful, nothing happens. The work goes on. But, if resources are scarce, those charged with financial administration cut back and the denominational offices get reorganized. As we said at the beginning of this section, when it comes to building a structure, most actions are regressive rather than progressive, and we believe that within this dynamic, denominational professionals have done remarkably well over time. We return to restructuring in chapter 6, "Incidents of Renewal."

Organizing religion in America is something about which many laypeople are ambivalent. It is the problem of church leaders. Creating structures for mainline denominations is caught in a history that has never come to grips with the twin values of efficiency and a heartfelt faith. Put another way, the structures of mainline denominations are caught between identity and mission.

An implication and a question present themselves at the close of this chapter on handling the "fragments of fragments." One senses in this highly selective but, we hope, trustworthy rendering of how denominations came to be and what they do, a remarkable resiliency. Running through the analysis is a capacity to adapt, adopt, and survive in the midst of ebb and flow. The Rumor is misleading, partly because it focuses on a too-recent period of denominational history—usually since 1965—while being largely ignorant of or unwilling to take into account, a longer and deeper look at what denominations have accomplished and how they developed. Awe, not obituary preparation, might be the appropriate response.

3. A BEWILDERING COURSE OF EVENTS

The modern man is in general, even with the best will, unable to give religious ideas significance for cultural and national character which they deserve.
—Max Weber, 1958

Denominations come in here: they can serve as reminders and agents of something larger.
—Martin Marty, 1991

An American Community

In the 1730s, religious people in the New World longed for a heartfelt faith and they found it in the midst of mass revivals. At the beginning of the twenty-first century, religious people in the New World still long for a heartfelt faith, but today, they are more likely to find it on their own. For a heady moment in American history, from roughly the 1900s until the 1950s, the leaders of the mainline denominations believed something different was afoot and that they were at the center of it. The mainline denominations were well positioned in the society and were convinced they could make a difference. The leaders believed they were at the forefront of the dawning of a new "American Community" based on the pursuit of peace and justice for all Americans. (The phrase an "American Community" is our creation.) Perhaps the idea of an American Community was naive, or maybe it was simply the audacity of people who thought too highly of themselves. In any case, the pursuit of an American Community was short lived as the more powerful forces of world history and American religious individualism reasserted themselves.

It is reasonable to think of American history as the story of a people teetering between chaos and order. America wondrously holds together, but it does so mysteriously, often appearing one misstep from disaster. The historian Gordon Wood (1993:359) describes America in the early nineteenth century as "a society of plain, ordinary people all busy pursuing their own private interests." He (1993:359) continues:

> But, it was increasingly clear that no one was really in charge of this gigantic, enterprising, restless nation. Government was weak, the churches were divided, and social institutions were fragmented. Nevertheless, "order" somehow seemed to "grow out of chaos," and people guided themselves "without the check of any controlling power, other than that administered by the collision of their own interests balanced against each other."[1]

To the founders, America became, in very short order, a country other than the one they had envisioned. They believed that "eminent men and imaginative minds" were in control of events and caused things to happen. "But the American Revolution had created 'something like a general will,' in which the course of society was shaped 'less by the activity of particular individuals' and more by the 'mass of intellectual, moral and physical powers'" (Wood, 1993:360). In this world, public opinion became the arbitrator of truth. Public opinion became "the truth." "In no country in the world did public opinion become more awesome and powerful than it did in democratic America" (Wood, 1993:364). America was to find greatness by "creating a prosperous free society belonging to obscure people with their workaday concerns and their pecuniary pursuits of happiness—common people with their common interests in making money and getting ahead" (Wood, 1993:369). America was free and enterprising, but not without its costs—"its vulgarity, its materialism, its rootlessness, its anti-intellectualism" (Wood, 1993:369).

Religious leaders in America, perhaps more than religious people in general, have often wondered what to do with America the ordinary. On the one hand, the country offered and delivered immense political and social freedom and the potential for gaining great economic wealth, but at the same time it made truth into public opinion and it mercilessly and wantonly used many, if not most, of its "weaker" citizens as grist for the great economic mill. What was (is) America? What is a society that is held together by little more than an infinite number of personal interests realized as transactions intended for personal gain? Much was made of the myth of American values, democratic or republican principles, the rule of law, even the reign of God, but ordinary America, the America that mattered, ran on a lower plane. Jefferson wrote the words. Americans had the inalienable right to "life, liberty, and the pursuit of happiness." Americans took that to mean they had the right to be left alone with their own economic interests with as little interference as possible. It was sometimes called freedom. Could such a place be a society, much less a just society? What could be made of a people that decided the truth, and right and wrong for that matter, by a preponderance of public opinion? There had to be something more, something else to hold it together, something to make it an American Community where people felt and acted for more than themselves and their own interests. In an American Community people would care about each other; they would reach out to the least of these and do right by them.

But, as the country moved from the eighteenth to the nineteenth century and on toward the Civil War, there appeared to be too much ordinary interest wrapped in bitter national sectionalism. In the South, there was slavery and in the North there were urban problems, which were simply under better cover in the rural areas. Shops were giving way to factories and as they did, a laboring "class" was being born and it was a class more difficult to control. Religious denominations, instead of addressing the issues that stood in the way of national unity, were ready and eager to take up sides. In the churches, the profane mixed uncomfortably with the sacred.

"Reform," particularly in the industrializing North, became a watchword, and it was the Christian (Protestant) social reform movement that set out to treat the more egregious social sores. Causes were easy to come by—public schooling, the abolition of imprisonment for debt, the passage of a mechanics lien law,[2] prison reform, the rehabilitation of prostitutes, and the building of hospitals for the insane (Wallace, 1972:383). The Christian reform movement managed to pull together coalitions and get some things done. But the coalitions had little life beyond a single cause. Once some progress was made, the fragile coalitions often disbanded.

By the end of the Civil War, the economy of the South was in shambles. In the North, the rich got richer while the ranks of the poor multiplied exponentially. A thousand new immigrants grasped for the same menial jobs. Labor was cheap and, by the law of supply and demand, people were barely paid enough to support life. Still the masses came, boat after boat, including for the first time a large number of Roman Catholics. Teaching people to be "Americans," to value democratic processes and the rule of law, to adjust to factory life, to live moral lives when government was weak and the controls of the European class system were an ocean away, became a preoccupation of religious leaders and their political counterparts.

In the 1920s, there were basically two Protestant camps. In one were the conservative, "fundamentalist" evangelicals who were convinced that reform depended on the salvation of souls and modern science would be the end of religiousness. In the other camp were the more liberal religious denominations that were taken by the Social Gospel. For the leaders of these denominations the relationship of faith to science, particularly social science, was less troubling, even exciting. If science, including social science, could point to some general principles that could be used to make life better, then science was a welcome ally. If, in the hands of some, science cast doubt on a literal reading of the first chapters of Genesis, then so be it. As theologian John Cobb (1991:Part II. Paragraph 11) describes it, the position in the mainline, which became widely shared, was that "the Bible could be read as the evolutionary or progressive discovery of the truth about God, a truth that is quite compatible with biological evolution. This truth about God could also be integrated with the thinking of the Social Gospel and the findings of the students of religious experience." After the Scopes Trial in the mid 1920s, the fundamentalists were on the run and the mainline leaders took center stage.[3] They may have been outnumbered, but they were much closer and more acceptable to the centers of social, political, and cultural power.

The Congregationalists, Episcopalians, Presbyterians, Methodists, American Baptists, Disciples of Christ, and the United Lutherans "represented well over half the constituency of the Federal and National Council of Churches, supplying an overwhelming amount of their leadership, and to an amazing degree dominating the various enterprises ancillary to the main conciliar organizations" (Hutchinson, 1989:4). In other words, the leaders in these denominations were running the show when it came to respectable, legitimate religion in American society. They were the action. They were America's recognizable and accepted religious face. The fundamentalists stayed well out of sight, not to be heard from again until the neo-evangelicals tied their comeback to the more accommodating celebrity of Billy Graham.

Most of the leadership of the mainline churches did not consider themselves "liberal" or even "modernists." When forced to choose, however, they were clearly not in the fundamentalist camp. Instead, they were more likely to think of themselves as "evangelical, confessional, progressive, or moderate" (Hutchinson, 1989:10). Holding to these values, they thought they had found a way to negotiate the more corrosive aspects of modernity. Their denominations operated as modern institutions and they increasingly adopted corporate models as the national offices grew. They had found a more modern way to read the biblical text. But, perhaps more than anything else, what united them was the belief that "they bore the heaviest responsibility for guiding the nation, sustaining both its moral vision and its watchful walk along the paths of righteousness" (Gustad, 1989:23). They were responsible for an American Community.

What *was* an American Community? Perhaps the most representative voice of the mainline, the editors of the *Christian Century* (a confident title for a magazine) felt the basis of this community was a common commitment to a wholistic society that was guided by the pursuit of peace and justice for all Americans. It was biblically based and focused on the Jesus of the Gospel accounts. It was ecumenical. It was white and middle class. In style, it was polite, circumspect, well-mannered, and tolerant. It sought to be prophetic but it was often content in taking a more centrist path that was more in tune with the rank and file as they built homes in the suburbs. The mainline leaders believed that an American Community was embodied in the unity of their denominations. Modernity had made its move. It was both wonderful and terrifying. Modernity's "isms" (e.g., communism, unregulated capitalism, and fascism) had been completely discredited, so something new, something more than individuals pursuing their own interests, was needed—and it was available. The mainline leaders were responsible for cultivating and extending this vision. Again, as Cobb (1991:Part II. Paragraph 5) describes it:

> A good many pastors discovered that the individualistic approach simply did not touch the real suffering and injustice that the industrial revolution brought with it. To save individual souls and leave this suffering and injustice unchanged could not, they believed, fulfill their calling to serve Christ. Returning to the Synoptic Gospels, they saw that at the heart of Jesus' message was the Kingdom of God. They interpreted this to be an earthly society in which God's will is done. And they found much Biblical support for the view that God's will is justice and social righteousness. The radical conclusion that they drew is that the salvation proclaimed by the gospel is first and foremost the salvation of society as a whole. Individual salvation has its meaning and place only in relation to that!

I think it was the last period in our national history in which being a Christian and being at what was felt as the cutting edge of fresh thinking and social transformation went easily together for large numbers of young people—and adults as well. The belief that the twentieth century would be the Christian century was convincing and did not feel oppressive or imperialistic. The Student Volunteer Movement attracted many of the leaders on college campuses to give their lives, often in other countries, to bring to them a Christianity committed to justice.

Looking back, the values embodied in an American Community were always more hope and dream than reality. Evidence that there was little of an American Community was always easier to come by than evidence it existed. After fifty years, the response of the mainline leaders to what they perceived as threats now appear reactionary, instead of progressive. For example, in an editorial of June 13, 1951, the editors of the *Christian Century* attacked pluralism, which they believed worked directly against what they were trying to achieve. The mainline rhetoric of today is awash with the praises of pluralism, though many of the mainline denominations struggle under the weight of it. (See chapter 6 for ways the denominations are responding to pluralism.) But, to the leaders of the mainline churches in the 1950s, pluralism was wrong. It stood in the way of an American Community. To them, pluralism meant "a columned life—a republic with complete and separate institutions for, say, Protestants and Catholics and Jews. Fearing that Catholic schools would form a strong base for a subculture, and worried about the decline of the public schools as the junior wing of American public religion's informal church establishment, the editors reared up" (Marty, 1984:980).

Writing about the editors, the historian Martin Marty (1984:980) continues:

A nostalgia similar in ways to that of today's religious New Right was evident in the magazine. In the good old days, the editors believed, Americans spoke "the same language" and had "the same cultural background," as well as many other important "sames." The editors still favored immigration quotas to limit the lumps of peoplehood that could not be blended into homogeneous America. For a long time the system had been successfully digestive; it could cope with non-Protestants as impotent minorities. But now Catholicism was large and powerful, with leaders who would "like to alter certain of the basic concepts upon which American democracy is founded." This was not quite the old nativism; the editors had no heart for that. Yet they could not swallow the changes easily.

Borrowing definitions from J. S. Furnivall, the editors of the Christian Century thought pluralism was comprised of "two or more elements that live side by side, yet without mingling, in one political unit." Such a society can have "no common will"; anomie and instability will result, with union built only on fiscal concerns or national defense. How then to express a social will? How to be other than vulnerable to communist or other ideological propaganda? Blaming Catholics for the proliferation of Catholic parochial schools, labor unions, civic clubs, veterans' organizations and political lobbies, the editors feared that Protestants would compensate with their own self-interest groups. The editors did not notice the extent to which these already existed, and that, in a way, they were speaking for what no longer was the "same" America, but one particular set of interests. Yet through all these years in subtler editorials and choice of articles, they showed awareness of that changing world.

If the hopes of the country were on the shoulders of the leaders of the mainline denominations, they stumbled and fell even as they continued to act as if they stood upright. "Needless to say this apparently successful wholistic vision and practice was exceedingly fragile" (Cobb, 1991: Part II. Paragraph 13). It was based on a series of ideas that proved wrong too often. Because of their belief in the progress of Western history, that Christianizing the society could provide a solution for all problems, that education would lead to the discovery and acceptance of the "truth," and that human rationality could open all doors, mainline leaders "overplayed" their hand.

Mainline leaders found it difficult to admit that America was not particularly enthusiastic about or committed to an American Community. The evidence suggests that as they pursued their goal, they never were "in touch" with the wider American milieu. Regular people, if they were interested in religion at all, longed for a heartfelt faith that was highly personal, and they wanted it for themselves, not a wider community. What was all this ambition for a peaceful and just society? As long as an individual was free to pursue personal peace and affluence, what more was possible? Who really cared about an American Community but the religious elite?

As it turned out, the mainline religious leaders were in no better touch with the emerging, most critical elements in American (via Europe) thought. For these academic (and activist) voices, the idea of an American Community was built on a much too optimistic view of American society. To these emerging voices, the vision was both oppressive and reactionary. It was too middle class. It was too white. It was one step away from domestic colonial imperialism. An American Community was a vision that never had a chance.

On the Defensive

The hopes of the mainline leaders collided with the reality of the decade of the 1950s. The 1950s led down a dark hallway of locked, soon-to-be unlocked, closets of racism, sexism, and classism. On the one hand, the United States stood alone with the industrial capacity and economic wealth to create a new middle class leaving behind the industrial cities with their factories and cathedrals, to build single family homes in pristine farm fields spread out along an ever developing interstate highway system. America had survived the Great Depression and been victorious in two world wars. The United States had saved the world and restored the possibility of freedom and democracy. The Christian (Protestant) faith had survived while the ideologies of the world had been defeated; well, except for communism.

Despite these successes, the United States was facing off with an emerging nuclear power intent and aggressive in exporting its own ideology. The Soviet Union and its new Chinese surrogate were willing to support insurgent Communist uprisings wherever they could be found. Just when the world seemed safe, it turned out to be more dangerous than ever. Direct confrontation between the superpowers raised the prospect of nuclear annihilation.

> The fact is that America in 1950 was not only troubled in the soul at the same time it was building countless new suburban churches to bring in the young families looking to be fed, it was also profoundly weary on a level having to do with spiritual creativity. It had few truly new ideas, nor did it want them; it wanted only to recover to the religion of times past, changing the trappings enough to suit a world of cars, TVs, and consumer culture (Ellwood, 2000:9).

The mainline churches were reduced to trying to hold on. Here is a list of the ways the world fell apart as it slid through the 1950s into the 1960s, taking the values of the American Community with it.

1. The ideal of a wholistic society of peace and justice for all Americans that was polite, circumspect, mannered, and tolerant collapsed amidst the fear of Communists, the invasion of South Korea, and the pervasive threat of nuclear war. And then, there was the unavoidable, more clearly revealed reality of ongoing and entrenched racism and segregation.
2. The government—always suspect—was both accused of being full of Communists and/or willing to allow "witch" hunts of possible

Communists. Even the conservative Army General turned President, Dwight D. Eisenhower, warned of the power of the military, industrial complex. In the South, state governments were openly resisting attempts to address American apartheid. In the major metropolitan cities of the North, city governments were dominated by corrupt political machines more intent on maintaining their systems of patronage than in meeting the needs of the citizens. In short, "government" could not be trusted.

3. Big business was not trustworthy either. Books on the "organization man" were bandied about by the popular press. For example, David Riesman's *The Lonely Crowd,* William H. Whyte's *The Organization Man,* and C. Wright Mills' *White Collar.*

4. Evangelicals reasserted themselves, seeming to appear out of nowhere. They returned to holding mass revivals and seemed to control a surprisingly well-developed set of institutions including colleges, seminaries and mass media outlets. These evangelical voices stood squarely in the conservative political camp.

In short, the hope of an American Community collapsed. The fractious lines in the society and in religion defined themselves ever more clearly, with liberals siding with liberals and conservatives siding with conservatives.

Back to the Future: Individualistic, Popular Religion or a Community of Faith?

Since the collapse of hope for an American Community, the mainline denominations have struggled to come to grips with their place in American society. There are seven books which we have found instructive about the mainline's role in American society. Published between 1972 and 2000 (although Robert Ellwood's work published in 2000 is really about the 1950s), they will be presented in roughly chronological order. It is interesting to note that some of them play off each other. That is, they critique each other either directly or indirectly and although selective, these seven are fairly representative of the help available in understanding the mainline's relation to society. For other observations and advice, see the references used in describing the various forms of The Rumor in the Introduction of this book. What follows is a list of authors, ordered by publication date, with a key word or two about their "message."

1972	Dean Kelley—Strict churches grow.
1986	Robert Bellah et al.—What ever happened to community?
1988	Robert Wuthnow—Individualism is winning.
1994	Dean Hoge, Benton Johnson, and Donald Luidens—There are new fluid boundaries.
1999	Wade Clark Roof—It is a spiritual marketplace.
1999	C. Peter Wagner—It is a new Apostolic Reformation.
2000	Robert Ellwood—The 1950s were the crossroads.

Dean Kelley's Strict Churches

Beginning as early as 1972 with Dean Kelley's *Why Conservative Churches are Growing*, those who write about American religion have pointed to a decline in membership among mainline denominations. Most often, mainline denominations have been accused of being out of touch with, and unable to meet the needs of, the American masses. Kelley (1972) held that the mainline denominations had neglected the most important religious question regular people ask related to "ultimate meaning." The mainline religious leaders, as we have shown, were interested in working for an American Community, but Kelley is no doubt correct, that goal is perhaps not personal enough; too out of touch with the long and well-established preference of Americans for a heartfelt faith. Kelley reiterates his argument in the Preface to the paperback edition of *Why Conservative Churches Are Growing*. He offers new support for his thesis by citing survey research on the most important tasks of the local church from the point of view of laity. Kelley organizes the items into two groups. The first group includes (in order): winning others to Christ, providing worship for members, providing religious instruction, providing ministerial services, offering the sacraments. The second group, again in order, includes: helping the needy, supporting overseas missions, serving as a social conscience of the community, providing fellowship activities, and maintaining facilities for the congregation. Supporting the denomination is in eleventh place. Kelley's point is that conservative (strict) churches grow because they most confidently, directly, and succinctly address the items in the first group. Put another way, conservative churches grow because they put individuals first and the wider community second. Conservative churches grow because they openly embrace the heartfelt.[4] Even amidst the renewed social activeness of some conservative evangelicals, their first religious instinct is individualistic and personal. Nothing could be closer to the "heart and soul" of conservative evangelicalism than the phrase, "You need a personal relationship with Jesus."

The lists can, however, be read in two ways. Is winning others to Christ only a personal matter? Likewise, is worship only about an uplifting personal experience? Religious instruction can be much more than successful, personal living. Ministerial services can be more than attending to personal needs. If the community was considered more important, these items would take on a different look. Winning others to Christ would be about being together, while following Jesus is about reaching out to "the least of these." The communal act of worship could only be done in the midst of a community because it is about community and its relationship to God. Religious education in this community would be about learning and carrying on the tradition, and tending to the grand narrative of the community of God. The sacraments would become entry into the community and would express God's commitment to us through the church.

Robert Bellah's Habits of the Heart

Bellah (with considerable help from his documents research team) the strong strain of individualism in American religion, but he interprets it in a challenging way:

> The community exists before the individual is born and will continue after his or her death. The relationship of the individual to God is ultimately personal, but it is mediated by the whole pattern of community life. There is a givenness about the community and the tradition. They are not normally a matter of individual choice. For Americans, the traditional relationship between the individual and the religious community is to some degree reversed. On the basis of our interviews, we are not surprised to learn that a 1978 Gallup poll found that 80 percent of Americans agreed that "an individual should arrive at his or her own religious beliefs independent of any churches or synagogues. . . ." This is a strange statement—it is precisely within church or synagogue that one comes to one's religious beliefs . . . " (Bellah et. al., 1986:228)

There's the issue. The relationship between the person and the religious community has been reversed! Most Americans seem to agree that the individual is prior to community. This view is not logical or experiential. (Who of us arrives on the scene without community and tradition?) But it is one of those assumed "common sense" understandings of what it means to be an American.

Bellah's work clearly shows "a bewildering course of events" (Bellah et. al., 1986:237). That course of events includes:

- mainline denominations trying to "do more" than emphasize internal over external religion
- offering a conception of God that is more than "a higher self" and is involved in time and history
- presenting a picture of living "a biblical life in America"
- seeking to be a "community of memory"
- treating biblical and historical sources with "intelligent reappropriation" rather than "literal obedience"
- relating Christian faith and practices to all of contemporary life—"cultural, social, political, economic," and not only to personal and family morality
- steering a course between "mystical fusion" with the world and "sectarian withdrawal" from it
- operating near the "center of American culture"
- having intellectuals who speak "for the church" to the wider society
- segregating scientific knowledge from knowledge gained through "faith, morality, and art"
- failing to provide a "Tillich or Niebuhr" as a catalyst for addressing church or society

And, what is the aftermath of this course of events? Bellah doesn't mince words:

> Without the leavening of a creative intellectual focus, the quasi-thera-peutic blandness that has afflicted much of mainline Protestant religion at the parish level for over a century cannot effectively withstand the competition of more vigorous forms of radical religious individualism, with their claims of dramatic self-revelation, or the resurgent conservatism that spells out clear, if simple, answers to an increasingly bewildering world (Bellah et. al., 1986:237).

Robert Ellwood's 1950s: Crossroads of American Religious Life

It is not only Bellah who makes the point that the community of faith, much less the wider community, takes a distant back seat to more individualistic conceptions of the faith. The religious historian Robert Ellwood (2000:7) points to the 1950s as a time when "popular" religion focused more on personal needs than on "high brow" alternatives, such as social issues, peace, and justice. Popular religion longed for "an imagined time somewhere in the past when faith could be simple and pure, when families were loving and together, and when emotions better than those evoked by the war could be freely felt and expressed." Ellwood (2000:7) continues:

Like popular religion generally, faith in the bookstores and at the feet of the popular preachers in 1950 was faith more of images than of ideas. Above all, it was personal, seeking to appropriate the power and faith of the past in a way accessible today for oneself, one's family, one's career, one's world. The mavens of popular faith were well aware of this. Note the frequency of the words "you" and "your" in the previously mentioned book titles.[5] The intellectual theologians talked about "man"; the populists about "you."

In the mainline denominations, there was a clear split between the liberal, social reform minded, seminary trained clergy and the members of their congregations. Ellwood (2000:110) contrasts Reinhold Niebuhr and Norman Vincent Peale:

> To many white, middle-class Americans and their churches—though certainly not to African Americans or other minorities, or to still exploited ranks of laborers, housewives, and children—it seemed that by 1950 nearly all the big battles for social justice had been won. The terrible evils represented by the Axis side in the victorious but exhausting war had been defeated; social security was in place; and wages were rising. Even in regard to race, many told themselves, slow progress was being made. It was now time to turn inward and see how newly affluent people could live full and fulfilled spiritual lives.

Ellwood (2000:194) adds that this intensely personal emphasis corresponded well with an increasing "compartmentalization" of modern life, and a reemerging conservative "evangelicalism" that went hand in hand with a renewed emphasis on "free enterprise." Like Bellah, he wonders if the mainline denominations are simply "overmatched." "In retrospect it is clear that evangelicalism, boasting individualism, experience-orientation, quasi-anti-institutionalism, and deep roots in the American past, has assets the alternatives could not match" (Ellwood, 2000:194).

Robert *Wuthnow's* The Restructuring of American Religion
Wuthnow (1988:55) also highlights the absence of an acknowledgment of "community" in contemporary descriptions of the function of religion in society.

> Descriptions of religious bodies often paid little or no attention to such vital aspects of its functioning as fellowship, mutual caring and sharing, the collective enactment of religious rituals, or the cultivation

of moral obligations through actual experiences of bonding and reconciliation. In place of these, emphasis was placed primarily on the spiritual growth of individuals. The corporate body became subtly transposed in a service agency for the fulfillment of its individual members. This tendency . . . was, however, rooted in relatively well established religious traditions.

In short, "how to empower the individual to be morally committed was more the issue than how to construct moral community itself" (Wuthnow, 1988:56). Conservative clergy, and those in the mainline with their ears to the ground, knew that faith based on the community would inevitably give way to religious forms giving voice to deep inner emotions and that "an outmoded social gospel" would give way to "a message of personal redemption" (Wuthnow, 1988:57). The possibility that a religious group could do something collectively—something that really mattered for the well being of all—receded to obscurity.

Wuthnow concludes that the idea of community failed to capture the imagination of Americans. This failure, along with rising levels of income, education, and mobility, eroded the sense of loyalty people felt to denominational families and their distinctive voices.

Hoge, Johnson, and Luidens's Vanishing Boundaries

Dean Hoge, Benton Johnson, and Donald Luidens extensively review the hypotheses of mainline decline in their book, *Vanishing Boundaries* (1994). Their analysis is based on telephone and personal interviews with a nationwide sample of persons between the ages of thirty-three and forty-two (in 1989) who had been confirmed in Presbyterian churches. They conclude that:

1. Youth counterculture of the 1960s is not a major source of mainline Protestant decline (Hoge, Johnson, and Luidens, 1994:176). They do not, however, dismiss the long-term impact of cultural changes that the 1960s typified. They also question the impact of anti-institutionalism (1994:176).

In our survey and in other research we saw evidence of this attitude, usually couched in terms of rejection of large, impersonal, out-of-touch organizations. We found relatively few Boomers who expressed hostility toward the church itself. We did discover a generalized lack of interest in denominational or ecumenical organizations or their various projects. Rather than being anti-institutional, our respondents tended to see large-scale organizations as irrelevant to their religious lives.

2. Membership losses in the mainline denominations are also not related to more "liberal" social policies of denominations. Hoge, Johnson and Luidens (1994:178) note: "[We] are convinced that the basic reasons for membership decline have little to do with the issues highlighted in the ongoing conflict between liberal and conservative factions in the mainline denominations. . . ."
3. Kelley's proposition that mainline churches are "weak" is essentially correct. (They also point out, however, that several conservative and "presumably strict" Presbyterian denominations also have lost members during most of the twentieth century.) The problem, according to Hoge, Johnson, and Luidens (1994:191), is mainline theological liberalism.

> For several decades the major branches of Presbyterianism were dominated by traditionalists, but during the 1920s, liberals, in alliance with the more numerous moderates, laid the groundwork for the increasing prevalence of modern theological views that occurred in the decades that followed. The posture of Presbyterian seminaries, theologians, and officials shifted toward an affirmation of critical scholarship, modern science, and the historical relativity of religious thought and practice. Although some of today's Presbyterian leaders have theological positions that are decidedly conservative, most of them do not. As a result of the liberal drift, Presbyterians no longer learned much from their ministers and Sunday school teachers about the historic doctrinal standards of the church. Moreover, liberals put little emphasis on sin, judgment, and the necessity for redemption, preferring instead to emphasize ethics and Christian service. This shift was a welcome relief to many within the churches who considered the old doctrines burdensome and distasteful, but the new themes tended to blur the old distinction between the Christian life and the life of "good people" who are not Christian. Liberalism did not offer compelling reasons why nonbelievers should make a profession of faith.

We are left, apparently, with what the baby boomers are interested in buying:

1. Religious education for their children.
2. Personal support and reassurance. "They need a place where they can pull their lives together, where they can get away from their home or workplace for reflection and reinvigoration" (Hoge, Johnson, and Luidens, 1994:204).
3. Social contact and sense of community.

4. Inspiration and spiritual guidance. "People sought inspiration from the Bible and from worship services. They needed worship to be uplifting and empowering, drawing them away from petty concerns to remember the larger picture, out of self-pity to praise, adoration, and thanksgiving. They wanted devotions and music to be encouraging" (Hoge, Johnson, and Luidens, 1994:205).

Being uplifted and encouraged, raised out of self-pity to praise, adoration, and thanksgiving is quite a distance from a commitment to the hard work of living together in a society intent on dividing itself up into smaller and smaller insulated and isolated segments. The "bottom line" is that boomers want to be inspired. We ask: Inspired to do what?

Wade Clark Roof's Spiritual Market Place

Wade Clark Roof worries (like Weber before him) that there may be nothing that transcends these individual pursuits of a heartfelt faith. He describes the state of religion as a "spiritual market place." The very idea of community is called into question. The shift has occurred in the move from the modern to the postmodern world where everyone invests in themselves, essentially by themselves, making utilitarian, short-term alliances when they show some instrumental value. "Disenchantment" with organized religion has set in. People are not turning to other institutions, but are "turning inward in search of meaning and strength" (Roof, 1999:57). People "hope that their own biographies might yield personal insight about the sacred." Theology has been "democratized." People are not left only to choose from the established doctrines and theologies; they are creating their own. It is as if we have been transported back to eighteenth-century America.

Roof makes a distinction between what he calls ordinary religion, expressed in such things as nature worship, holiday rituals, sacred myths, and healing practices; and extraordinary religion, which is characterized as more "formal and institutionalized." It is more visible and identifiable. It is more like supernatural theism. "Historically, forces have pulled the two types of religion apart" (Roof, 1999:63). Protestantism became demythologized in its encounter with modernity, but in the process religion became "other," separate, or disconnected from daily life. Now people are looking to find something more relevant, more connected and whole. Mainline Protestantism contributed to its own decline by teaching young people to "rely upon their conscience and to think for themselves about moral and religious matters" (Roof, 1999:64). Faith became a matter of psychology and the arbitrator of truth was no longer public opinion but one's own personal experience. Roof (1999:67) again states: "Not surprisingly, 'How can I feel good about myself?' emerged as a far more pressing question to many Americans than 'How can I be saved?'" Finally, the last ingredient of this change is the media, particularly the Internet and immediate access, literally, to the wide world of ideas.

Religious institutions, not just the mainlines, find themselves on the short end of the stick. In a survey, over half of the population agreed "that churches and synagogues have lost the real spiritual part of religion." In Roof's research, this sentiment was no more likely to be expressed by members of the mainline congregations than it was by members of the "strict" churches (Roof, 1999:85). And, now, the "real spiritual part of religion" is defined as its personal and psychological impact. If this is the "real spiritual part of religion" then the mainline denominations haven't lost it; they never had it. "In effect, what has long been understood to be a latent, undisclosed consequence of churchgoing—psychological benefits—had become the manifest reason for religious participation" (Roof, 1999:86). In this environment,

> preaching skills and leadership styles are especially important given that popular faiths in this country have been, and still are, largely revivalist, emphasizing grace, hope, and a deeply personal relationship between the believer and God. A play upon these symbols is almost a guaranteed success on the American religious stage, and the plays have been, and continue to be, amazingly innovative in their narration and pitch to human needs, hopes and aspirations (Roof, 1999:87).

The popularity of conservative evangelicalism lies not in the faith or the morality that it teaches, but "in its attention to personal needs" (Roof, 1999:129). This theme will surface again in the work of our next commentator, C. Peter Wagner. These findings begin to explain the difficulties oldline conservative evangelicals are having as reflected in the end of *Moody Magazine,* for example.

Roof, however, is not willing to run down the road with Bellah, which is the road we have taken, that individualism is the enemy of religious institutions. He (1999:152) notes: "Individualism is more than a one-way influence shaping styles of institutional commitment; it also opens up new possibilities for religious institutions and changing modes of personal commitment." People who switch often enter the new group with higher levels of commitment, for example. "Much energy is expended in creative realignments of belief and practice by individuals on the move, and there is also a corresponding energy on the part of religious and spiritual leaders attempting to reach people in their new settings" (Roof, 1999:154). Roof (1999:158) continues:

Fears that expressive individualism is destroying institutional loyalties are easily exaggerated and distract from its positive values for genuine religious conviction. Individualism also makes possible an affirmation of religious faith, identity, and belonging as self-chosen. And as a result, people often possess a greater clarity of their own beliefs and metaphysical views as well as a sense of personal accountability; contrary to the view that individualism only erodes commitment, it can actually "tighten," and not just "loosen" ties to groups and institutions.

What values, however, will people use as the basis of their decisions? It is not just the choice, it is the criteria used for making the choice that matters. Roof (1999:159) maintains that people are making these choices based on "feelings." "Feelings and inner satisfactions thus become an added force in the sifting and sorting of religious choices." As to any sort of community, Roof (1999:163) notes that "networks" have substituted themselves for neighborhoods. These networks are "communities focused around, most notably, self-expression and nurturance, group sharing, and helping others." All of this is done within, not outside of the context of self-interest and the parameters of one's own personal experience.

Roof (1999:305) concludes his discourse, noting: "The nagging question throughout our analysis remains: What about spiritual depth and its power to transform individuals and society?" He argues that the baby boomers are gaining "spiritual maturity" and points to two "centers of value." These are: (1) "defining love as mutuality in marriage, family, and intimate relations" and (2) the environment. It appears to us that these centers are, at best, weak if one is concerned about spiritual depth and the power to transform individuals and society. Roof searches to find, amidst what appear to be his doubts, something positive about all this.

Because much of popular spirituality is highly personalized and largely dependent on the individual's own private or small-group practice, it has the advantage of being highly adaptable in a mobile world where people's lives change often, yet suffers from a lack of long-term, shared face-to-face exchanges among its followers. Such exchanges are crucial for their reinforcement of individual commitments. Spiritual seeking suffers from another problem as well. Research evidence suggests that intense, instrumental approaches to spirituality—that is, wanting the benefits of believing but in the absence of strong convictions about such beliefs and practices—can be self-defeating. Without some level of commitment, spiritual seekers are likely to remain tourists and never become pilgrims (Roof, 1999:307).

Tourists. Never Pilgrims. These findings give great pause to those who hope for a community that transcends the heartfelt. The point here, however, is that this "new" approach to religion is simply a variation on the heartfelt of old. It is this form of religion that religious leaders have found themselves up against since the founding of the republic. One option is to go with it—to make the most of it. But, in our humble opinion, going with it takes us nowhere new and nowhere worth going.

Peter Wagner's New Apostolic Reformation

Peter Wagner (1999), unlike the other authors cited in this chapter, has been willing to venture an alternative to denominations. In Wagner's view there is a "New Apostolic Reformation" underway. The new apostolic reformation is made up of "interdenominational networks" led by megachurch pastors and by the senior pastors of other large, but not quite as large, congregations. These congregations are highly visible within the denominations, if they have a denominational affiliation, and they are at the center of "extradenominational networks." These networks are groupings of congregations where "anchor churches," along with the pastors of surrounding congregations, "network together for the benefit of the whole city" (Wagner, 1999:30–31). It is Wagner's view that congregations will flow into and out of the networks as they feel the need. Issues of ordination, which contributed to the rise of traditional denominations in the first place, are handled by local congregations as they see fit.

The new networks are determined to avoid rules and regulations which, as we have pointed out, are at the very foundation of denominations. The question, then, is how some level of order can be achieved, and this is a question that Wagner, to his credit, does not completely avoid. He takes the very American view that congregations should be left alone to make their own choices (exchanges) and in time, all will work out for the best. Wagner (1999:127) rejects the sociological notion that charisma, if it is to survive the passing of its source, is always routinized.[6] Instead, he believes that the apostolic network will stand or fall on "personal relationships," which admittedly will limit them in size. Yet even though individual networks may be relatively small, there still can be thousands of them. Still, the question of "power and authority" in this free church tradition undoubtedly plagues the future of the new apostolic reformation; therefore, it is our belief that if the networks are to survive over the long run there must be routinization.

Despite Wagner's hope that the new apostolic network will eschew control, there is the assumption that some level of order will be achieved through a set of shared, core values and beliefs. Wagner avoids setting these out as "givens," but he does note that among the congregations he considers key to the apostolic network, there are "generally agreed upon" positions that include the following:

1. The Bible is true and normative. It is the absolute authority for faith and practice.
2. Jesus Christ is God and Lord.
3. An individual's personal relationship with Jesus Christ makes the difference between heaven and hell.

Moral "non-negotiables" include:

1. Human life begins at conception.
2. Homosexuality is sin against God.
3. Extramarital heterosexual relationships are sin (Wagner, 1999:67).

Perhaps most revealing is Wagner's contrast of traditional beliefs with "the counterpart we are now observing in the New Apostolic Reformation" (1999:52) We use the entire list to show the current state of thinking among those who claim to know the most about popular religion in America and what, in that context, is most likely to have an impact in improving the competitive position of a congregation or denomination. Wagner claims to know what will work to draw in the masses. These emphases are remarkably *this*-worldly. Kelley's thesis was that people were most worried about questions of "ultimate" meaning and that the mainline had turned its attention too directly to the here and now. It is Wagner's view, on the other hand, that the mainline is too mired in the past and should "get with it." In the new apostolic network, a very traditional set of "core values and beliefs" (cited above) is set out alongside a remarkably postmodern shift in theological emphases. Here, the contradiction is resolved by understanding that the link is the *individualistic and personal*. In the new apostolic network, eternal salvation takes a back seat. Post-Christendom is, by this account, considerably more concerned for salvation in the here and now. What remains is not only personal, but also highly *instrumental*—using religion as a private, personal tool. To the extent that sin and guilt put in an appearance, they do so only as one passes on to victorious living. The more salient point is to get on to personal peace and affluence. Christ is less the Savior than Jesus is a mentor. Jesus is not the crucified one, but Jesus is glorified and sitting at the right hand of God. Wagner (1999:52–53) sees movement:

1. from Christ as Savior to Jesus as Lord
2. from Jesus the Lamb to Jesus the Lion
3. from the cross to the crown
4. from justification to sanctification
5. from saved from death to saved for life
6. from water baptism to spirit baptism
7. from living in the desert to crossing the Jordan
8. from saying prayers to praying in the spirit
9. from denying or fearing evil to doing spiritual warfare
10. from counseling to deliverance
11. from training to anointing
12. from guilt for sins to victory over sins
13. from liturgy to spontaneity
14. from singing in the choir to singing in the spirit
15. from pipe organ to keyboard
16. from hymns to praise and worship songs
17. from staff ministry to body ministry
18. from predicting to prophesying
19. from telling to showing
20. from seeing and hearing to discerning

Mainline Denominations Revisited

To assess the "bewildering course of events" that we have traced in this chapter, we call upon two voices: John Caputo and Dietrich Bonhoeffer. According to John Caputo (2001:31), the very essence of religion is the confession of love for something besides ourselves. We are religious:

> when we "bind ourselves over" to something other, which means something other than ourselves, or when we gather ourselves together and center ourselves on a transforming focus of our love. Something grander and larger than us comes along and bowls us over and dispossesses us. Something overpowers our powers, potencies, and possibilities, and exposes us to something impossible. Something makes a demand upon us and shakes us loose from the circle of self-love, drawing us out of ourselves and into the service of others and of something to come. The religious sense of life kicks in when I am rigorously loyal, "religiously" faithful to the service of something other than myself, more important than myself, to which I swear an oath, which has me more than I have it.

If we use Caputo's phrase "more important than myself," we are compelled to conclude that the move from a modern to a postmodern era has produced little progress. The grand idea of moving beyond ourselves is buried by more powerful forces in American history and religion. Mainline congregations and denominations conspire against themselves in an attempt to become more like the religious groups that have broad appeal. They struggle with their identity and their place in American society. They fall from the "establishment" even as they attempt to exercise responsibility for it. They work for an American Community only to hold on for dear life as the society fragments around them taking their youngest members with it.

Have there been times in the history of the Christian Church, when, using the words of the authors we have reviewed, the church wasn't "up to it," or "no match for," or "lacked the assets" to address its situation? Bonhoeffer's travail took place during one of those times. Bonhoeffer largely predicted Hitler's intention of waging war and his attempts to exterminate the Jews, but he found himself helpless to stop it even as he played a role in the unsuccessful plots to assassinate Hitler. In his helplessness, Bonhoeffer tried to make sense of the past and to think through what future Christianity might have, if it was to have a future at all. From prison he wrote to his friends and family about what had gone wrong. He contrasted what he called "religion" with faith. The characteristics he attributed to religion—the religion of Christianity that had failed in his time—are instructive. What Bonhoeffer detested most was the depiction of a God who was increasingly being pushed out of the center of things. In his July 8, 1944, letter from prison, he wrote, "I want to start from the premise that God shouldn't be smuggled into some last secret place . . ." (Bethge, 1971:346).

Bonhoeffer's main biographer, Eberhard Bethge (2000:873–877) identifies seven characteristics of Bonhoeffer's concept of religion, or of a church that "wasn't up to it." These characteristics include:

1. Metaphysics. Assigning God a "religious" role rather than an all-encompassing role in the world.
2. Individualism. "The tendency to direct one's gaze to the private human sphere and cultivate the salvation of one's own soul."
3. Partiality. The increasing restriction of faith from areas of life "explained" by science and human ingenuity to areas as yet "unexplained."
4. Deus ex Machina. The idea that there must be a supreme being "so that we can be rescued from dangers, have our mysteries solved, and hear

our questions answered." "This idea makes religion an escape from real life and from mature responsibility for it."

5. Privilege. The assumption that Christianity was a "class" thing for the "higher" classes or that the church required a privileged position in the society from which to operate.
6. Guardianship. The protection of people who haven't quite grown up, perpetuating a maturity-killing dependency.
7. Dispensability. The antidote to religion's penchant to perpetuate its role as necessary by confusing its temporality or penultimate forms with ultimate matters of substance.

What is the result? In Bonhoeffer's words, "The church on the defensive. No taking risks for others" (Bethge, 2000:875). From the point of view of John de Gruchy (1991:38), one of Bonhoeffer's long time interpreters, Bonhoeffer knew that individualism was both a powerful and dangerous force.

> He [Bonhoeffer] gave specific content to this [his analysis of the failure of religion] by defining it more precisely as a form of individualism and a metaphysical system. Religious individualism made human beings abscond from their responsibility for the world, and its attempts to provide a schematic and secure answer to the search for salvation enable men and women to avoid the direct challenge of the gospel.

The mainline denominations tried, at least for a brief moment, to think about an American Community. We know this work was too narrowly conceived and full of self-interest. But, at the same time, we see no cause for rejoicing in the current state of affairs. There is very little evidence that other religious groups in America have the interest, will, or the faintest of abilities to pursue a greater vision. We write in the hope that the mainline can recover something special, its memory. From this memory, something of significance can be built. At the very least, people in mainline denominations can see in their spirituality something more than a means to personal peace and affluence.

A clue to the future of mainline denominations is in paying attention to writers like Caputo ("something other than myself") and Bonhoeffer ("The church on the defensive. No taking risks for others."). Gazing into the "private human sphere" is too small a vision to interest God and believers, either old or new.

4. NUMBERS

Take a census of the whole congregation of Israelites.
    —Numbers 1:2a

The Israelites did just as the Lord had commanded
Moses. They camped by regiments and they set out
the same way.
    —Numbers 2:34a

T he occasion of the above census is instructive.
    As the people of God prepared to move into a
    new place in geography and history, God
ordered that a statistical assessment be done. Part of their
spiritual preparation was to answer the question, "What
do the numbers say?"

    In this chapter we will provide an assessment—not
divinely ordered—of the numbers relevant to understanding denominations today. We have created three charts on
membership change and financial giving that tell the story.
Then we will review some of the newest survey research.
The Rumor of the imminent demise of the mainline

denominations is never far from our minds as we think through the meaning of these numbers. The accepted wisdom is that the mainline denominations are weak and getting weaker. It is our view, however, that mainline denominations have never really been that strong, despite brief appearance at center stage from about 1920 through the 1950s. Mainline denominations have *always* been somewhat distant and remote from the heartfelt religion of regular people, so this is nothing new. Mainline denominations have often wanted something more; something we have called an American Community. The reality of this distance is our starting point.

Readers whose eyes tend to glaze over at the specter of charts and graphs may want to skip to the "What Do All These Numbers Say" section starting on page 108. But you will miss something: a clear look at the face of several denominations in the family photo album of denominations. There are some interesting comparisons to be made.

Winners and Losers in Early America

The work of sociologists Roger Finke and Rodney Stark (1989, 1992) has done much to give historical perspective. They believe that from the earliest days of the American Republic the oldest religious denominations—Congregationalists, Episcopalians, Presbyterians—kept their distance from the "free marketplace" of heartfelt religion created by the work of revivalists in America. According to Finke and Stark's (1989:29) not-too-flattering account,

> the idea of appealing for members was alien to organizations accustomed to severely limiting the active involvement of the laity. Moreover, the highly educated and dignified clergy who controlled these denominations disdained the vigorous marketing techniques employed by the upstart evangelicals; they viewed the informal religious practices of the frontier with contempt and distanced themselves from the common folk; the latter responded in kind.

Those upstart sects both created and supplied the kind of religion that appealed to regular people. It was the Methodists and the Baptists who were most in touch with what people wanted, and so it was that the Methodists and the Baptists grew phenomenally.

The account of the numbers is convincing. Heartfelt religion is *the* American religious form, and when it comes to the religious marketplace, the Methodists and the Baptists dominated. At their height, the Methodists had more than ten million members, and the Baptists may have had nearly 25 million. None of the other mainline religious groups comes close to the Methodists, much less the Baptists. In fact, the sum of the members of what today are the United Church of Christ, the Presbyterian Church (U.S.A.), the Episcopal Church, and the Evangelical Lutheran Church in America at their height in the 1960s was still about five million less than the number of Southern Baptists over the same years. And there is more to this numbers story than simply an accounting of the winners and losers. Because of the phenomenal growth of the U.S. population overall, *the losers still won.* They may have disdained the religious marketplace, but the Congregationalists, the Episcopalians, and the Presbyterians, and later the Lutherans, still grew in membership. They did so decade after decade throughout the nineteenth century and into, and through, the middle of the twentieth century. America was growing so fast it could support and supply new members to all the churches.

Members and Money in the Modern Era:
1940 to 2000

As noted above, the membership growth for all the mainline denominations in America continued in absolute numbers through the 1960s. Between 1940 and 1960, the Methodists added over 2.5 million new people to their membership roles and the Lutherans (ELCA) nearly two million people. The Presbyterians increased almost 1.5 million. Even the smaller United Church of Christ added half a million. Looking back, we now know that things were about to change. The Methodists, the Presbyterians, and the United Church of Christ didn't make it through the 1960s without losses, and by 1980 the number of people leaving or being removed from the roles of these mainline churches was significant. But from the view of the past, only the most insightful or lucky prognosticator could have predicted that turnaround. For the first time, there were winners and losers based on the absolute totals (see Table 1).

Even if the religious leaders could have anticipated that the growth would end, it is unlikely they would have acted differently. After all, there was an enticing allure of growth through the nineteenth century and into much of the twentieth century. Religious *unity* was also in the air. Holding back would have run against both history and the spirit of the times. There was much to do beyond the congregations, and the congregations had their hands full. Why not support the work of their denominations? The national offices took on more and more responsibility for producing congregational resources, working for social justice, creating and supporting social ministry,

Table 1: Membership Change by Decade after 1940 for Selected Denominations						
	1940–1950	1950–1960	1960–1970	1970–1980	1980–1990	1990–2000
Assemblies of God	119,644	190,124	116,425	439,463	1,117,012	396,058
Church of Jesus Christ of Latter-day Saints	386,913	375,573	586,269	737,854	1,456,000	941,827
Evangelical Lutheran Church in America	864,882	1,312,994	354,635	-265,866	-143,532	-114,820
Episcopal Church	421,030	851,861	16,501	-499,822	-339,954	-112,723
Presbyterian Church (U.S.A.)	519,666	951,225	-116,452	-683,322	-514,649	-322,107
Roman Catholic Church	7,350,423	13,470,022	6,109,829	2,235,113	8,118,173	5,115,015
Southern Baptist Convention	2,130,715	2,651,702	1,896,441	2,172,094	1,238,283	921,899
United Church of Christ	269,272	263,716	-260,526	-244,364	-137,032	-221,892
United Methodist Church	1,609,724	988,132	-132,112	-989,791	-734,272	-444,181

Source: *Yearbook of the American and Canadian Churches,* National Council of Churches of Christ in the U.S.A., 1990, 1992, and 2002.

extending global mission, and so on. If anything, getting big was too easy, too affordable. As a percentage of total income, congregations supported denominational work at about the same level they always had.[1] The percentage of congregational money given to denominational benevolences varied within a small percentage range until recently. The pie just got bigger and bigger (see Table 2). The absolute amounts of money for benevolences also increased dramatically. According to Wuthnow (1988:99):

> Over the years, growth in memberships, generalized affluence in the economy at large, and inflation rates have combined to greatly increase these [denominational central office] budgets in absolute terms. And in absolute terms, denominational hierarchies have been able to sustain a larger variety of functions fulfilled by a larger number of professional staff workers. In relative terms, though, the central budgets have not expanded.

Table 3 displays an annual average change in dollars for denominational benevolences over a fifty-year period. For example, every year between 1951 and 1970, the Presbyterians had an increase of nearly $11.4 million in contributions to benevolences. Every one of the denominational

Table 2: Gifts for Denominational Benevolence Budgets as a Percent of Total Giving*								
	1925	1932	1940	1951	1970	1980	1990	1999
Presbyterian	18.9%	16.1%	19.0%	18.6%	18.9%	20.9%	16.2%	14.2%
Methodist	18.6%	17.4%	13.5%	15.7%	17.6%	23.2%	21.9%	21.9%
Lutheran	24.5%	20.9%	17.4%	22.2%	19.2%	16.9%	13.4%	10.4%
Congregational	13.3%	13.3%	12.5%	12.5%	14.8%	13.7%	11.9%	9.8%
Baptist	21.1%	16.2%	16.4%	16.5%	15.5%	16.1%	14.7%	12.9%
Episcopal	14.1%	5.7%	12.5%	14.8%	15.9%	15.7%	15.7%	15.7%

*Because of mergers over the years, these statistics are based on the combination of the major religious groups within a denominational family. As a result, for example, the Lutheran group includes the current Evangelical Lutheran Church in America and its predecessor bodies, and the Lutheran Church–Missouri Synod. Congregational includes the United Church of Christ and its predecessor bodies. (Statistics are not available for 1960.) Source: *The Handbook of the Churches*, Federal Council of Churches of Christ in America, 1925; *The Yearbook of American Churches*, Federal Council of Churches of Christ, 1933, 1941; *The Yearbook of American Churches*, National Council of Churches of Christ, 1952; 1972; *The Yearbook of the American and Canadian Churches*, National Council of Churches of Christ in the U.S.A., 1982, 1992, 2001.

groups experienced increases throughout the period. But by 1970, at least for the Presbyterians, Lutherans, and Congregationalists, the percentage given to benevolences began to fall. The "strict" Baptists held off the declines until the 1990s, as did the Methodists, but between 1990 and 2000 all of these religious groups found themselves losing rather than gaining members. The money, following membership growth and decline, rose and fell within the course of fifty years.

Table 3: Changes Per Year in Gifts to Denominational Benevolences over the Period* (in millions, adjusted for inflation)				
	1951–1970	1970–1980	1980–1990	1990–2000
Presbyterian	$11.4	–$2.6	–$0.9	–$1.2
Methodist	$18.6	$16.4	$13.7	–$25.6
Lutheran	$13.4	–$5.1	–$9.1	–$8.4
Congregational	$2.8	–$2.4	–$0.3	–$2.4
Baptist	$18.8	$36.6	$3.9	–$2.2
Episcopal	$4.1	$4.3	–$8.4	–$3.0

Source: *The Yearbook of American Churches*, National Council of Churches of Christ, 1952; 1972; *The Yearbook of the American and Canadian Churches*, National Council of Churches of Christ in the U.S.A., 1982, 1992, 2002. *See note on mergers for Table 2.

In the Reagan years, the ethos of institutional distrust, with its roots in the late 1960s and 1970s, finally worked its way through all of society. Support turned to skepticism and then to cynicism,[2] and three developments within the mainline denominations, long well under way, made their presence felt. First, the membership base of the mainline was seriously eroding. A significant proportion of the baby boomers raised in church simply quit coming. Second, the members who were left gave less, not more, for denominational benevolences. Third, congregations in the mainline denominations began to keep a larger proportion of their total giving for congregational purposes. These last two points were certainly as true for the "strong" Baptists as they were for the "weak" mainline churches.

Denominational Strength in Diverse and Inclusive Communities of Faith

"Denominational Ties Still Bind, Study Finds." That headline or similar ones appeared in many of the nation's newspapers in March 2001. The interfaith survey "Faith Communities Today" (FACT), involving 14,301 congregations in forty-one denominations or faith groups, produced some findings that differ from The Rumor literature.[3] For example, Dudley and Roozen (2001:17) note that "sociologists report that denominationalism is declining in significance for congregational identity. But 62 percent of congregations say they reflect clear expressions of their denominational heritage." This expression of denominational heritage is even stronger in congregations with a distinctive racial, ethnic, or national identity. The finding clearly calls into question the belief that a denominational connection is no longer important to a majority of congregations. Dudley and Roozen (2001:2) also point out that "the great majority of faith communities are vital and alive" and are "making major contributions to the welfare of their communities through a combination of social and spiritual ministries." What we are primarily interested in here is the distinctive impact denominations have on members as well as congregations. We believe that this impact can be much stronger than it currently is in mainline denominations, if they focus on the importance of their traditions as diverse and inclusive communities of faith. We suggest that it might be possible to find strength in something other than relying on a certain set of doctrinal beliefs and using them to indoctrinate. Perhaps members don't have to share completely doctrinal beliefs if they hold a common commitment to being part of a *Christian community* that puts the emphasis on making life better for all. Mainline denominations have not invested nearly enough in exploring alternative ways of achieving strength.

As a way of starting a discussion about alternative sources of strength, we would like to disagree with the idea that where beliefs are concerned, the members of mainline denominations are exceedingly different from those in conservative denominations. Sure, differences exist, but simplistic schemes that label all members of strict denominations as conservative and all those in the mainlines as moderate or liberal are exactly that—too simple. We believe denominations are much more interesting and complex, and suggest that the gulf between "strict" conservative churches and the mainline churches isn't as great as one might think.

What follows is a snapshot of denominational identity based in large part on FACT data and data from a second, complementary project called the *U.S. Congregations Survey*.[4] In some respects, Lutherans closely identify with Episcopalians, while in others, they are more akin to the Southern Baptists! It is challenging to sort through all the facts and figures, but by doing so, new possibilities may present themselves and new conclusions may be reached.

Doctrine and Identity

It could be expected that denominations impact individual religious identity in a major way. Religious researchers have often searched and found evidence of such a connection, but it has never been as clear as some have suggested. Denominational religious leaders and most local clergy hope to shape a core religious identity. But some denominations are much more concerned than others about shaping a distinctive religious doctrinal identity. In some ways, mainline denominations have actually worked against being distinctive, and toward a more ecumenical vision.

Studies of religious beliefs were an important component of the assessment of mainline denominations as weak religious institutions. In the earliest survey work, members of mainline religious groups were more likely to support the "radical theological reformulation of the twentieth century," while in such denominations as the Southern Baptists the "rank and file seem almost unanimously committed to the traditional faith of their fathers" (Glock and Stark, 1968:55). It was work in the early 1970s, however, that promoted and popularized the view that broad support for less orthodox religious views was evidence of denominational weakness (Kelley, 1972). The main thesis was that mainline religious groups had lost their sense of meaning and, with it, their will to impose or to demand high levels of commitment. According to Dean Kelley (1972), religiousness that stressed reason and tolerance without requiring conformity to rigid standards was well on its way to no religiousness at all. "Social strength and leniency do not seem to go together" (Kelley, 1972:83). By definition, then, there was no such thing as a "strong" ecumenical religion. Strength was exclusive to exclusiveness, and strong religious groups were those that "try to impose uniformity of belief and practice among members by censorship, heresy trials and the like" (Kelley, 1972:26). Without a widely shared sense of exclusive truth, there was also no convincing case for proselytizing. Or, to put it another way, for religious groups with strength as an agenda, diversity was a serious liability.

A host of other researchers have stated or adopted some version of this thesis (Finke and Stark, 1989, 1992; Iannaccone, 1994; Hoge, Johnson, and Luidens, 1994). We, however, don't want to accept it so quickly. We want to call some parts of the thesis—particularly the suggestion that shared conservative doctrinal beliefs are the only source of denominational strength—into question. Even the details of the thesis do not hold up so well. Most recently, a series of studies have shown that among the strictest religious groups, members are much more likely to hold diverse views than one might expect (Davis and Robinson, 1996; Hoffman and Miller, 1997; McConkey, 2001). Only the members in denominations at the extremes of the liberal-conservative denominational continuum hold very similar beliefs, while among the moderate or middle religious groups there is a broad spectrum (Gay, Ellison, and Powers, 1996). With regard to denominational affiliation and social and political beliefs, Jewish groups and unaffiliated persons are the most liberal, and the Southern Baptists and members of other fundamentalist, evangelical, and charismatic groups are the most conservative. These groups, the ends of the continuum, are denominations that promote an exclusive point of view. But, between these "ideological poles," there is "a sizeable center consisting of Catholics, Methodists, Presbyterians, and Lutherans" (Gay, Ellison, and Powers, 1996:8). This is a *center* not because religious commitment has deteriorated into nothingness, but because people *within* these groups have different understandings of the faith and different ways of working out their relationship to it. There are conservatives and liberals *in* mainline denominations, not just liberal or conservative denominations.

Much of the conflict in mainline denominations is precisely because they are not homogeneous. The vast majority in denominations are moderates, but there are also substantial minorities of liberals and conservatives. Put differently, what makes a mainline denomination mainline is its ability to include rather than exclude. If the point is to define a narrow "core" and convert people to it, then mainline denominations will never be strong. But if the goal is a Christian community where people are committed to something other than themselves, then making the provision for diversity is a good place to start. If mainline denominations have failed, it is in not being demanding enough about a commitment to Christian community as a major expression of what it means to be a Christian.

Lutherans and Southern Baptists

We know the Lutherans best. As the transplanted American version of the Scandinavian and German state churches, the membership of what today is the Evangelical Lutheran Church in America for a long time consisted largely of persons of Scandinavian or German heritage, living in relatively self-contained communities in the South, East, and Midwest. Within those communities, Lutherans tended to see membership as inclusive rather than exclusive. Baptism was the means of entry into the church, and it was available to all. The clergy may have engaged in intense doctrinal debates, but over time those debates gave way to a longing for Lutheran unity. Different ethnic sensibilities, along with varying pieties, ended up alongside one another. Accepting the Augsburg Confession, "rightly" preaching the Word, and administering the sacraments was important, especially to the well-educated clergy, but uniformity, or enough uniformity among the members, beyond baptism, was generally understood as ensuring that everyone could assent to the Creeds or recite Luther's Small Catechism. Considerably more room was given when it came to religious experience. This tendency to define the parameters of religiousness broadly around a core *is* the major impact of the denomination. We cannot overstate the extent to which we see this tendency as an essential building block for Christian community. This community may be weak on doctrinal boundaries, but this weakness is only a problem if no other boundaries have been defined. There is no reason that the level of commitment to the community, as opposed to agreement on narrowly defined doctrinal positions, cannot serve as the basis for strictness.

The problem is that the level of commitment to the community has not been understood or articulated as a boundary issue. People say they are Lutheran because they attend a Lutheran church or, even if they currently do not attend, they were baptized in a Lutheran church. That is not enough. They are, however, very likely to accept basic Christian teachings. They are likely to go to church and to pray regularly. They are likely to put an emphasis on the graciousness of God. But within this context, they do not consistently espouse positions that are narrowly "Lutheran," and it is our view that this is not a significant problem. The problem is a lack of commitment to a Christian community that demands that we live together, working out our differences and supporting each other as we follow the example of Jesus.

The first empirical studies of religious commitment conducted with members of the Lutheran Church in America (one of the predecessor bodies of the ELCA) in the late 1970s and early 1980s showed considerable diversity in the midst of high levels of agreement on "the core elements" of Christian belief. Wuthnow (1983:31) writes:

> As far as the core elements of Christian belief are concerned, therefore, the evidence suggests both consensus and relatively high levels of commitment. Despite this consensus, it is also readily apparent from the data that much diversity exists. Only a handful of the laity happened to give the same response that the theologians had chosen as the most adequate or accurate statement on all ten of the confessional belief questions (2.6%, to be exact). Most of the laity held other views on at least some of the questions. For example, sizable numbers leaned more toward a concept of faith that emphasized "trying to do what is right" rather than viewing faith simply as trust in God's grace. On questions about the sacraments, some held that these were essential to salvation, others that they were valuable but not essential, and still others that they were merely traditions of the church. Other questions revealed difference of opinion on the nature of biblical inspiration, on beliefs about life beyond death, and on attitudes toward conversion.

Wuthnow (1983:52) continued:

> One conclusion that can be drawn from these findings is that there is as much doctrinal diversity among active laity as there is among less active members. The reason why some persons hold views that differ from the predetermined confessional response concerning faith, their relation to God, or the sacraments is not that they are marginally involved in the church. Even the most actively involved are likely to differ in their specific doctrinal views. By implication, the results also suggest that doctrinal diversity is probably accepted, and perhaps reinforced, among those who participate in the activities of the church. If there were strong pressures to conform to a particular orientation, it would seem doubtful that active participants would express other views as frequently less active participants do.

This broadly inclusive approach to the faith *is* the Lutheran pattern. In short, when it comes to boundaries, the doctrinal positions of laypersons will give us little to work with. Perhaps most illustrative are the differences among the members on key issues of the Bible. Twenty-four percent of ELCA Lutherans say the "Bible is the Word of God to be taken literally, word for word." This is not the position of most clergy, where doctrinal boundaries are set out much more clearly. The denominational tendency, stated in the *Confession of Faith* of the ELCA *Constitution,* is toward a more contextual approach to biblical interpretation, and 27 percent of the members say the "Bible is the Word of God, to be interpreted in light of its historical and cultural context" with another 43 percent responding that the "Bible is the Word of God, to be interpreted in light of its historical and cultural context and the Church's teaching."[5] In other words, the members show a much broader range of views than the clergy. There appears to be no intention on the part of the clergy or the denomination to ensure that they do otherwise. Instead, the point should be to include those with different opinions and to model a community with room for differences. What matters is not one's view of the Bible, but the way a person lives in, and participates in, the Christian community. But these demands—the demands of community life—have not been emphasized nearly enough by mainline churches.

This broadly inclusive approach to doctrine is clearly evident in member responses to the question about their level of agreement with the statement that "all the different religions are equally good ways of helping a person find ultimate truth." Thirteen percent of Lutherans strongly agreed and 43 percent agreed. On the other hand, 18 percent disagreed and 7 percent strongly disagreed. Again, the responses of members do not follow those of the clergy (see Table 4).

For Lutherans the liberal-to-conservative continuum normally used to classify denominations in America manifests itself *within* the denomination, which is also the case for the Presbyterians. Among Southern Baptists, however, the doctrinal boundaries appear to be tighter, but there is much more variation than one might expect. Seventy-one percent of Southern Baptists say they believe that "the Bible is the word of God, to be taken literally, word for word." But 29 percent of Southern Baptists do not take the Bible literally word for word.

In fact, the percentage of Southern Baptists going "against" the dominant denominational paradigm is nearly the same as the number of Lutherans who go against the dominant paradigm (the 24 percent who say the Bible should be taken "literally word for word" plus the 6 percent for the three categories of the "not the word of God/ancient book" respondents.)

Table 4: Views of the Bible by Denomination						
	Lutheran (ELCA)		Presbyerian (U.S.A.)		Southern Baptist	
	Members (N=43,463)	Clergy (N=410)	Members (N=587)	Clergy (N=725)	Members (N=20,000)	Clergy (N=124)
The Bible is the word of God, to be taken liter-ally word for word.	24%	3%	18%	4%	71%	48%
The Bible is the word of God, to be interpreted in the light of its his-torical context.	27%	55%	37%	54%	17%	50%
The Bible is the word of God, to be interpreted in the light of its his-torical context and the Church's teaching.	42%	39%	38%	36%	11%	2%
The Bible is not the word of God, but con-tains God's word to us.	4%	3%	5%	5%	1%	0%
The Bible is not the word of God but it is a valuable book.	1%	0%	1%	0%	0%	0%
The Bible is an ancient book with little value today.	1%	0%	0%	0%	0%	0%
Don't know.	2%	0%	1%	0%	1%	0%

Source: *U.S. Congregational Life Survey,* 2001.

In other words, these data point to the problem of quick generaliza-tions about denominations and the uniformity of their members' beliefs. ELCA Lutherans have an institutional structure that is as highly centralized as any in the United States. On the other hand, the Southern Baptists are relatively decentralized institutionally, but neither of these denominations is homogeneous. For Lutherans, there is no apparent desire to achieve homogeneity. And if the Southern Baptists are a good example of a strict church, even denominations that hope to achieve some level of homogeneity have a difficult time showing they have rid themselves of a substantial minority of dissenters. In the postmodern era, doctrinal purity will be an ever-more illusive commodity.[6] We think that denominations which define their boundaries primarily in doctri-nal terms will have to regularly *push* dissenters out. We believe that for mainline denominations, accommodating doctrinal differences while simultaneously demanding commitment to an inclusive Christian community is a much better way to go.

A Comparison of Clergy from Several Selected Denominations

Do not read this section (pp. 95-108) if you think there's a danger you will get distracted from our point on the necessity, within the mainline denominations, of the core value of Christian community. But here we want to show how the stereotypical understanding of differences among denominations sometimes just doesn't hold up well. If you choose to skip this section, move on to "Is Denominational Loyalty Fading?" on page 108. *Do* read this section if you are curious how a Lutheran may be closer to a Nazarene than an Episcopalian. Question: On what topic is a Nazarene minister closest to a Unitarian/Universalist minister than to anyone else?

Gregory A. Wills, writing on "Southern Baptists and Church Discipline" in the *Southern Baptist Journal of Theology* (2000), says:

> For more than twenty years voting majorities at the annual meetings of the Southern Baptist Convention have endorsed a "conservative" platform based on a commitment to the inerrancy of the scriptures. They have rejected the "moderate" platform based on freedom and toleration. The argument was not theoretical. The question at stake was whether the convention had authority to establish doctrinal boundaries—to enforce doctrinal orthodoxy as a condition of service as a trustee or employee of the convention's boards and seminaries. When convention majorities voted in favor of inerrancy, they asserted that the convention had authority to judge religious beliefs in its appointments. In our churches, however, we demonstrate considerable ambivalence toward asserting such authority. We want to make certain that our missionaries and seminary professors are orthodox in faith and pure in behavior, but we tolerate much lower standards in our churches. Pastors, missionaries, and teachers are rightly held to higher standards.

In its document on *Vision and Expectations–Ordained Ministers in the Evangelical Lutheran Church in America,* the Division for Ministry of the ELCA (1990) states:

An ordained minister of this church shall be a person whose commitment to Christ, soundness of faith, aptness to preach, teach and witness, and whose educational qualifications have been examined and approved in the manner prescribed in the documents of this church; who has been properly called and ordained; who accepts and adheres to the Confession of Faith of this church; who is diligent and faithful in the exercise of the ministry; and whose life and conduct are above reproach. A minister shall comply with the constitution of this church.

Early in our discussion, we pointed out that one of the main functions of a denomination, back to the earliest days, was to protect and pass on the traditions of the faith. Clergy were expected to represent their denomination's view of the "correct" teachings. As a result, we should expect to find clear differences *among* clergy of different denominations. Recent survey work, conducted by FACT and the *U.S. Congregational Life Survey,* gives us the opportunity to see the extent to which these differences actually exist. Depending on the question, we have the data for comparisons for Lutherans (ELCA), Episcopalians, Nazarenes, Presbyterians (U.S.A.), Southern Baptists, and Unitarian/Universalists. When there are data for members, they have been included.

Views of the Bible

We expect differences among clergy from different denominations on views of the Bible, but it pays to be cautious. Only 3 percent of the Lutheran clergy believe the Bible should be taken literally, while 55 percent believe it should be interpreted in light of its historical and cultural context, and 39 percent believe it should be interpreted in light of its historical and cultural context *and* the church's teachings. As expected, the Presbyterian and Lutheran clergy are very close in their views, but what is surprising and runs against the stereotypical view is the fact that less than 50 percent of the Southern Baptist clergy take a literal view of the Bible.[7] (See Table 4 on page 94.) Among the clergy of these three denominations, the *majority* of Lutherans (55%), Presbyterians (54%), *and* Southern Baptists (50%) believe that the "Bible is the word of God, to be interpreted in the light of its historical context."

We also expect Presbyterians and Lutherans to be more open to the value of different religions, and that is the case. Ninety-nine percent of Southern Baptists disagreed or strongly disagreed that "all the different religions are equally good ways of helping a person find ultimate truth." But 83 percent of Lutherans and 83 percent of the Presbyterians also disagreed or strongly disagreed (see Table 5). Members of Lutheran congregations (54%) are most likely to agree or strongly agree that "all the different religions are equally good," but a substantial minority of Southern Baptists (21%) also agreed or strongly agreed with the statement.

Table 5: Agreement with the Statement: "All the different religions are equally good ways of helping a person find ultimate truth."						
	Lutheran (ELCA)		Presbyerian (U.S.A.)		Southern Baptist	
	Members	Clergy	Members	Clergy	Members	Clergy
agree or strongly agree	54%	9%	33%	10%	21%	1%
neutral or unsure	1%	8%	25%	7%	14%	0%
disagree or strongly disagree	25%	83%	42%	83%	66%	99%

Source: *U.S. Congregational Life Survey,* 2001.

Authority

The clergy were asked, "How important are the following sources of authority in the worship and teaching for your congregation?" The sources included sacred Scripture; the historic creeds, doctrines, and traditions; the Holy Spirit; human reason and understanding; and personal experience. The response categories were "absolutely foundational," "very important," "somewhat important," and of "little or no importance" (see Table 6).

Table 6: "Absolutely Foundational" Sources of Authority in Congregational Worship and Teaching						
Authorities	Lutheran (ELCA)	Episcopalian	United Church of Christ	Southern Baptist	Nazarene	Unitarian/ Universalist
Scripture	86%	54%	52%	98%	95%	1%
Holy Spirit	61%	26%	16%	79%	87%	2%
Historic Creeds	37%	37%	6%	5%	9%	2%
Reason	9%	19%	9%	3%	6%	45%
Experience	8%	9%	6%	7%	17%	41%

Source: *Faith Communities Today,* 2000. (Items could be chosen more than once. Percentages do not total to 100.)

The Southern Baptist (98%) and Nazarene (95%) clergy were most likely to say that Scripture was "absolutely foundational" followed by the Lutheran (86%), Episcopalian (54%), United Church of Christ (52%), and the Unitarian/Universalist (1%) clergy.[8] The clergy from the Nazarenes (87%) were most likely to identify the Holy Spirit as absolutely foundational, followed by the Southern Baptists (79%) and the Lutherans (61%). The Lutherans (37%) and the Episcopalians (37%) were most likely to regard the historic creeds and doctrines as foundational. Reason

Figure 1: "Absolutely Foundational" Sources of Authority
(Circles represent the "Historic Creeds/Doctrines")

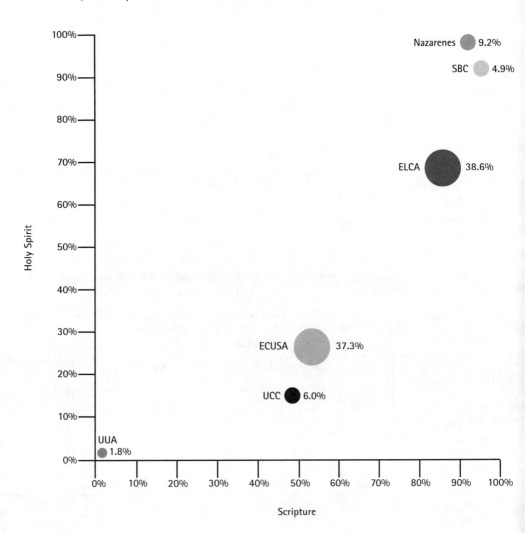

was most likely to be cited as absolutely foundational by the clergy from the UUA (45%), as was experience (41%).

This set of relationships can be shown spatially. Figure 1 shows each of the denominations based on the percent of clergy responding that the Holy Spirit, Scripture, and the historic creeds/doctrines were "absolutely foundational." While Figure 1 appears complicated, it is simply a picture of the material presented in Table 6. Views on the Holy Spirit are plotted along the vertical axis so that, for example, 2 percent of the UUA clergy indicated that the Holy Spirit was absolutely foundational, compared to 87 percent of the Nazarenes. Views of Scripture are plotted on the bottom axis. Again, 1 percent of the UUA clergy said Scripture was absolutely foundational, compared to 98 percent of the SBC clergy. Finally, the size of the circles reflects the percent of clergy who indicated that the historic creeds/doctrines were absolutely foundational.

Figure 1 reinforces, once again, the danger of quick generalization when it comes to denominations. Lutheran clergy have a high view of the authority of Scripture, even though they do not believe the Bible should be taken literally word for word. This "high" view of Scripture puts them more in the company of Southern Baptists and Nazarenes than it does Episcopalians or clergy from the United Church of Christ. On the other hand, when it comes to the authority of the historic creeds, Lutherans are more like the Episcopalians, and it is the clergy from the United Church of Christ who are more like the Southern Baptists and the Nazarenes.

The clergy were also asked to choose "the one source of authority that is most important in their congregation's worship and teaching" (see Table 7.)[9] Faced with this difficult decision, Scripture takes a predominate place as the most important source of authority for all these denominational

Table 7: The One Source of Authority Most Important in Congregational Worship and Teaching						
Authorities	Lutheran (ELCA)	Episcopalian	United Church of Christ	Southern Baptist	Nazarene	Unitarian/ Universalist
Scripture	82%	61%	78%	94%	70%	2%
Historic Creeds	6%	23%	5%	0%	1%	1%
Holy Spirit	11%	6%	6%	5%	27%	1%
Reason	1%	7%	9%	0%	0%	37%
Experience	1%	2%	3%	0%	1%	33%

Source: *Faith Communities Today,* 2000.

groups, with the exception of the clergy from the Unitarian/Universalists Association. Ninety-four percent of the Southern Baptist clergy chose Scripture as the most influential authority, followed by 82 percent of the Lutherans. On the other hand, Nazarene clergy (27%) were most likely to choose the Holy Spirit as the most important source of authority and 23 percent of the Episcopalians chose the historic creeds.

The Sermon

A sermon reveals the sensitivities of the preacher, and those sensitivities have a distinctly denominational flavor. Clergy were asked about the focus of sermons. "How often does the sermon in your worship focus on God's love and care, practical advice for daily living, personal spiritual growth, or social justice/social action?" (See Table 8.)

Of these four areas of focus, an emphasis on God's love and care is most likely to "always" be a part of a sermon in Lutheran congregations (66%). On the other hand, practical advice for daily living and personal spiritual growth are more likely to always be parts of sermons in Nazarene (69%) and Southern Baptist (67%) congregations. Social justice or social action concerns are much less likely to always be included as a focus of a sermon across the board.

Table 8: "Always" Included as the Focus of a Sermon						
Focus of Sermon	Lutheran (ELCA)	Episcopalian	United Church of Christ	Southern Baptist	Nazarene	Unitarian/ Universalist
God's Love and Care	66%	45%	4%	44%	36%	2%
Practical Advice for Living	17%	11%	16%	29%	29%	6%
Personal Spiritual Growth	26%	17%	18%	38%	41%	11%
Social Justice/ Social Action	4%	2%	5%	2%	1%	4%

Source: *Faith Communities Today,* 2000.

Again, we can show some of these differences spatially. Figure 2 is of the same design as Figure 1, but this time a focus on advice for daily living is on the vertical axis, a focus on God's love and care is on the bottom axis, and the size of the circles represents a focus on personal spiritual growth.

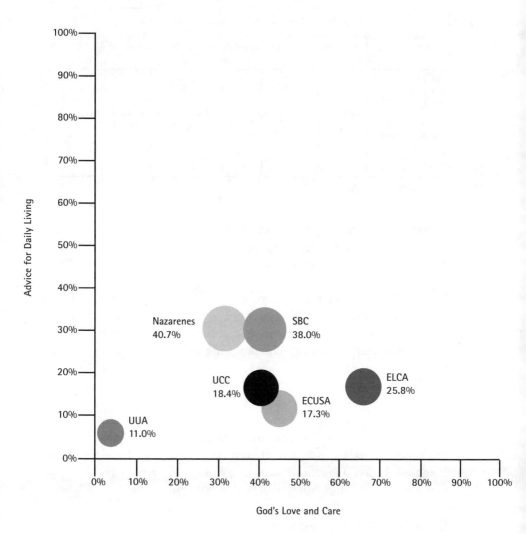

Figure 2: Focus of the Sermon in Worship
(Circles represent "Personal Spiritual Growth")

Advice for Daily Living (y-axis)

Nazarenes 40.7%
SBC 38.0%
UCC 18.4%
ECUSA 17.3%
ELCA 25.8%
UUA 11.0%

God's Love and Care (x-axis)

Creeds and Testifying

Clergy from denominations with a history of liturgical worship—the Episcopalians and the Lutherans—are much more likely to report the recitation of creeds or statements of faith during a worship service than those from Southern Baptist or the Nazarene congregations (see Table 9).

On the other hand, Nazarene clergy (59%) are much more likely than the others to report that they are more likely to always or often include a time for laypersons to testify about their faith.

Table 9: "Always" or "Often" Included in Worship						
Activity	Lutheran (ELCA)	Episcopalian	United Church of Christ	Southern Baptist	Nazarene	Unitarian/ Universalist
Recite Creeds or Statements of Faith	97%	98%	38%	7%	15%	62%
A Time for Lay-persons to Testify about Their Faith Growth	3%	5%	7%	28%	59%	28%

Source: *Faith Communities Today*, 2000.

Expectations and Enforcement

Clergy were asked: "Which one of the following three statements best describes your congregation?

1. Our congregation has definite expectations for members that are strictly enforced,
2. Our congregation has fairly clear expectations for members, but the enforcement of these expectations is not very strict,
3. Our congregation has only implicit/vague expectations for members that are seldom, if ever, enforced" (see Table 10).

Fifteen percent of the Nazarene clergy and 14 percent of the Unitarian/Universalist clergy reported that their congregations had definite expectations that were strictly enforced. Fewer than 3 percent of the Lutheran, United Church of Christ, or Episcopal clergy responded that they had definite expectations that were strictly enforced.

Personal Religious Practices

Clergy were asked about the extent to which personal prayer, Scripture study, or devotions; family devotions; fasting; dietary restrictions; abstinence from alcohol; activity restrictions on Sundays; and abstaining from premarital sex were emphasized by their congregation in worship and education (see Table 11). Ninety-three percent of the Nazarene clergy and 91 percent of the Southern Baptist clergy reported that personal prayer, Scripture study, and personal devotions were emphasized a "great deal" or "quite a bit" in their congregation's worship and education. This compares to 76 percent for the Lutherans, 70 percent for the Episcopalians, 64 percent for the United Church of Christ, and 14 percent for the Unitarian/Universalists.

Table 10: Expectations and Enforcement						
	Lutheran (ELCA)	Episcopalian	United Church of Christ	Southern Baptist	Nazarene	Unitarian/ Universalist
Definite Expectations/ Strictly Enforced	3%	2%	3%	9%	15%	14%
Fairly Clear Expectations/ Enforcement Not Very	51%	48%	42%	71%	79%	47%
Implicit-Vague Expectations/ Seldom if Ever Enforced	46%	51%	56%	20%	11%	39%

Source: *Faith Communities Today*, 2000.

Figure 3 on p. 104 shows the spatial relationship of these denominations. The vertical axis represents family devotions, the bottom axis represents Sunday activity restrictions, and the size of the circles represents personal prayer. What really separates the denominations is the matter of Sunday activity restrictions, emphasized by nearly 70 percent of Southern Baptist congregations, compared to less than 1 percent of the Lutheran congregations.

Table 11: "A Great Deal" or "Quite A Bit" Emphasis on Personal Religious Practices						
Personal Religous Practice	Lutheran (ELCA)	Episcopalian	United Church of Christ	Southern Baptist	Nazarene	Unitarian/ Universalist
Personal Prayer, Scripture Study, Devotions	76%	70%	64%	91%	93%	15%
Family Devotions	44%	32%	42%	32%	57%	2%
Fasting	1%	6%	1%	5%	18%	0%
Dietary Restrictions	0%	1%	1%	2%	4%	0%
Abstinance from Alcohol	3%	3%	3%	53%	61%	0%
Sunday Activity Restrictions	1%	27%	26%	69%	55%	3%
Abstaining from Premarital Sex	29%	18%	15%	76%	75%	2%

Source: *Faith Communities Today*, 2000.

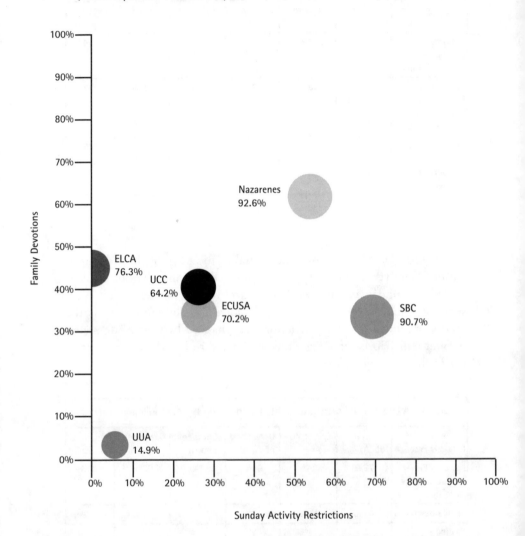

Figure 3: Personal Religious Practices
(Circles represent "Personal Prayer")

Family Devotions

Nazarenes
92.6%

ELCA
76.3%

UCC
64.2%

ECUSA
70.2%

SBC
90.7%

UUA
14.9%

Sunday Activity Restrictions

Figure 4 shows the spatial relationships of the denominations on the emphasis in worship and education on abstaining from alcohol (vertical axis) and abstinence from premarital sex (bottom axis), with the size of the circles representing fasting. In emphasizing abstention from alcohol and premarital sex, Southern Baptist and Nazarene clergy are closest. The Lutherans are the most likely mainline group to emphasize abstaining from premarital sex, while none of the clergy except the Nazarenes place much emphasis on fasting.

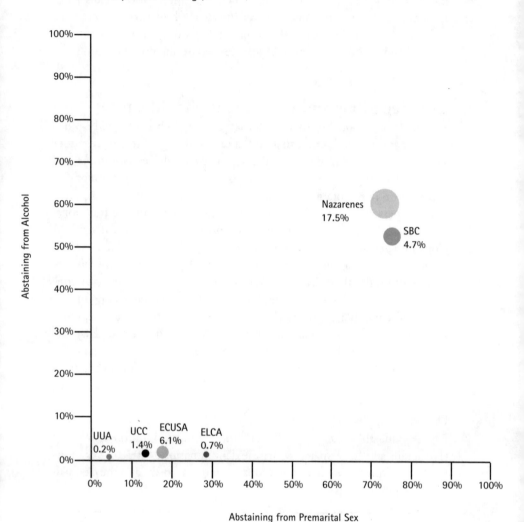

Figure 4: Personal Religious Practices
(Circles represent "Fasting")

Abstaining from Alcohol

Nazarenes
17.5%

SBC
4.7%

UUA
0.2%

UCC
1.4%

ECUSA
6.1%

ELCA
0.7%

Abstaining from Premarital Sex

An Observation

There is remarkable variation among these denominational groups in heritage, understanding of authority, and emphases in worship, education, and religious practices. Certainly, when it comes to a kind of personal piety based on abstinence, the mainline religious groups cluster together at one end of the continuum, with the Southern Baptists and the Nazarenes at the other. But *taken point by point,* it is nearly impossible to draw quick and easy generalizations. In terms of the authority of Scripture and the Holy Spirit, for example, the Lutherans are closer to the Southern Baptists and the Nazarenes than they are the Episcopalians. The Episcopalians and Lutherans, however, are close when it comes to the historic creeds and doctrines, and so on. In other words, differences among these denominations are not so clearly defined as one might expect.

Congregations and Denominational Identity

It would be reasonable to expect that congregations affiliated with a denomination would reflect that affiliation. With regard to congregations as institutions, many denominations provide model constitutions and expect their congregations to adopt an exact or "approved" version of that constitution to maintain affiliation. Congregations are also often expected to call a pastor approved by the denomination. These are the traditional and most direct ways that denominations bring some level of order to religious life. Yet, these efforts of denominations meet with limited success. Congregations, like their members, are often of their own mind, but the pattern of loyalty that exists does not follow a liberal-to-conservative continuum. Things are more complex. For example, the clergy in the Episcopal Church are most likely to say that their congregation expresses or celebrates its denominational heritage "very well," followed by the clergy from Assembly of God congregations (see Table 12). On the other hand, 27 percent of the clergy in United Church of Christ congregations responded that their congregation "slightly" or did "not at all" express or celebrate the denomination's heritage, followed by 14 percent of the United Methodist clergy and 13 percent of the Nazarene clergy.

Overall, the traditions that are most liturgical in their worship (Lutherans and Episcopalians), are the denominations with congregations that most express their denominations' heritage, according to the clergy in those denominations.

Table 12: How Well the Congregation Expresses Its Denominational Heritage							
	Assembly of God	Lutheran (ELCA)	Episcopal Church USA	Nazarene	Southern Baptist	United Methodist	United Church of Christ
Very Well	33%	26%	36%	17%	28%	14%	9%
Quite Well	36%	54%	43%	43%	39%	34%	29%
Somewhat	23%	16%	17%	27%	23%	38%	35%
Slightly/Not at All	8%	4%	4%	13%	10%	14%	27%

Source: *Faith Communities Today*, 2000.

Some congregations are more likely to purchase materials or supplies for worship, education, stewardship, or evangelism exclusively from within their denominations, but that is considerably more true of the Southern Baptists (33%) than the Nazarenes (19%) or the Assembly of God (18%) congregations (see Table 13). In general, the clergy from all these groups report a strong preference for denominational sources, except for those from the United Church of Christ.

Table 13: Where Congregations Purchase Materials or Supplies for Worship, Education, Stewardship, Evangelism, Etc.							
	Assembly of God	Lutheran (ELCA)	Episcopal Church USA	Nazarene	Southern Baptist	United Methodist	United Church of Christ
Exclusively from the Denomination	18%	4%	4%	19%	33%	12%	3%
Primarily from the Denomination	48%	69%	48%	64%	55%	55%	36%
Balanced Within and Outside the Denomination	25%	23%	41%	14%	10%	25%	41%
Primarily from Outside the Denomination	8%	4%	6%	3%	2%	7%	16%
Exclusively from Outside the Denomination	1%	0%	1%	0%	0%	1%	4%

Source: *Faith Communities Today*, 2000.

Finally, in terms of the level of a congregation's support for a denomination, the data are difficult to compare, because they are not systematically collected or reported. The situation improved somewhat with the crossdenominational work completed as part of the FACT project. We do know that giving to denominational offices has declined significantly since 1990. Lutheran (ELCA) congregations have the highest level of operating expenses (about 80% of total giving) and the lowest level of giving directly to the denomination (about 7% of total giving). Operating expenses seem to be lowest for the Southern Baptists (about 65% of total giving), while Southern Baptist congregational giving to the denomination is relatively high (about 11%). Among the Episcopal congregations, the operating expenses are about 75 percent of total giving, and giving to the denomination is about 10 percent.

Is Denominational Loyalty Fading?

Given the claims of The Rumor, that certain denominations are gaining at the expense of others, one might expect considerable switching of members from mainline denominations to those that are more strict. Are denominational loyalties weaker than in times past? Some take that point of view, but Reginald Bibby has taken another. Unfortunately, his research is often ignored, especially among those who perpetuate The Rumor—so we present a brief review of his findings here.

Bibby (1999) makes several important points. First, research and religious practitioners alike tend to "assume that identification without involvement simply doesn't count." Bibby (1999:152) counters: "What is perhaps rather remarkable is not that large numbers of North Americans identify but are not involved, but rather that they continue to identify even though they are not involved. . . . Psychologically, emotionally, and culturally, they continue to identify with religious traditions." Second, based on national, longitudinal survey data from Canada, Bibby (1999:155) concludes that comfort levels with other religious groups have increased, "but discomfort continues to exist, particularly as one moves further away from one's theological and cultural group home." Third, the problem for the mainline is that their members participated less, not an outright rejection of their religious roots. According to Bibby (1999:161), "ongoing identification has been accompanied by a psychological and emotional attachment to groups that clearly has outlived active participation." He (1999:161) concludes: "If groups can get in touch with such people, explore their interests and needs, and respond with integrity to what they are hearing, there is good reason to believe that the participation levels of at least some of their affiliates will increase."

What Do All These Numbers Say?

Statistical assessments can be long and tedious, but they are also a means for orienting and a means of spiritual preparation. Where are we? How will we know when we have moved into a different territory? This review of the numbers helps us chase down The Rumor. Things always seem to be more complex than they first appear, but after this review, here is a list of what we think we know.

- Denominations work hard to form a special religious identity among their members, and there is evidence that members of these various religious groups do, indeed, have different beliefs. Clergy, however, are more likely than lay members to reflect a certain denominational tradition. The laity are more likely to pick and choose, which, when it comes to religion, is an American tradition. This picking and choosing by lay members from all denominations makes any easy generalization suspect, particularly the notion that denominations as a whole can be categorized from conservative to liberal and strong to weak. There are liberal Southern Baptists and conservative Lutherans. At the same time, Bibby's research has shown that there are *families* of denominations, and members are unlikely to move comfortably out of one family into another.

- A denomination is faced with negotiating the differences among its own members. The challenge is how to do this. One strategy—exclusion—is to define the boundaries narrowly so that anyone who disagrees is pushed out. Another—inclusion—is to define a narrow core that allows, even promotes, diversity around that core. Both strategies have serious limitations in a society where religion is a voluntary matter. Few people are willing to put up with serious constraints, and as people go their own way it is more and more difficult to maintain a coherent core.

- Dealing with the differences within denominations raises the concern about community and the role mainline denominations can play in negotiating the territory between exclusion and inclusion. Much greater attention needs to be given to building new communities that more creatively negotiate differences among members. If it is no longer possible to hope for an American community, the need to build a *Christian community* within the denomination is even more pronounced.

- Mainline denominations are on the downside of growth in members and money. But the way *back* to growth is neither through more exclusion or inclusion, but through a fuller understanding of identity and its relationship to mission. This interplay of identity and mission is what makes a community both possible and viable. People, who have a choice, need *a reason to be something*. That something defines the boundaries. Once they have found that reason and that something, reinforcement is needed, both in and through the mission.

- That something, for mainline denominations, should be as much action as belief. Action is a way of living that is part of a Christian community, within which people can reach out to one another and learn to live together.

5. BUILT TO LAST

*The denomination is an earthen vessel, full of
cracks and holes. But the church in the present day
unfolding of history needs such vessels, or something like them. Built into these denominations
that stand the best chance of enduring and surviving are mechanisms and impulses for reform and
renewal. Their significance is less one that can be
marked by "decline" and more by something that
sounds more simple but is deliciously more complex—"change."*
     —Martin Marty, 1991

T his and the following three chapters shift from
analysis to possibilities. This chapter on clues
from organizational perspectives is followed by
one on examples drawn from denominations that share
life and hope. Then we focus on a possible way forward
and conclude with worries, learnings, and strategies.

This chapter looks at denominations from the perspective of organizational studies. A few studies have

shed light on why some organizations last over time and others do not. How do denominations stack up against these findings? Denominations, in the middle of the twentieth century, became thoroughly rational bureaucratic organizations. It would have been difficult, if not impossible, to take another course. As we have tried to show, denominations were always about order, and the very reasons behind the expansion of their agency role were economy and efficiency—the point of rational bureaucratic forms of organization. We neither hesitate nor apologize for taking an organizational view of denominations designed to improve how they do their work, particularly with regard to their central offices. We believe in the value of these offices. We want to challenge the critics of denominations to come clean. If there is a better, more effective, more efficient way of doing the global mission of the churches than through denominational auspices, then the case should be made. If there is a better way of starting new congregations or providing congregations with programmatic resources than through denominational offices, then let's have at the debate. But we believe that, despite the shortcomings of denominations, the alternatives are even more problematic.

Denominations have to get better at staying focused and doing their core tasks. Without effective denominations, the future of American religion will likely rest in the outcome—or the debris left along the way—of a battle between conservatives and liberals (Wuthnow, 1993:156). The churches and America itself would be better off with more, not less, denominationalism. Here we explore the organizational literature that might be relevant to denominations as organizations, because we believe they do good work, even while improvements can and should be made.

It has been shown that there is a tendency among all organizations to move toward very similar patterns of organization (Powell and Dimaggio, 1991). No matter what the primary function of an organization, over time they all take on the same basic characteristics. Religious or not, what is true for one type of rational bureaucratic organization tends to be true of another. What happens, then, if we look at denominations through the lens of organizational theory and practice? What can we learn?

Organizational theory and practice, as conceptual fields, are vast and deep. There are academic departments of organizational behavior complete with empirical studies, professional associations, and refereed journals. There are also popular studies aimed at a wider audience, particularly those in management, who are responsible for the bottom line. The people who work in organizations—almost all of us—find ourselves the objects of the latest "discovery." This has led to the view—not without justification—that top executives jump indiscriminately from one effort to another as they disrupt and make work more difficult. A seemingly endless parade of hot recommendations makes its way into the circle of those who manage in businesses, government agencies, or nonprofits. After a few success stories are reported, most of the recommendations lose their luster—and effectiveness—and fade from public view, sometimes leaving behind a good idea or two and a host of never-reported failures. Most organizational cultures strongly resist change with highly developed and effective means for warding it off. The combination of those factors and the conclusion that nothing *really* works are characterized by phrases such as management's flavor of the month, management by fad, or quality improvement by slogan. The lineup of strategies is impressive, from total quality improvement and its many variants to corporate reengineering, to management by or through strategic planning, to organizational alignment, to self-organizing work groups, to—most recently—communities of practice.

We do not intend to contribute, at least intentionally, to this malaise. What we have in mind is modest. We quickly review the best of the popular organizational literature—work people may have read or heard about—and then we draw some conclusions. We have one goal. *We want to know why some organizations are successful over long periods of time and what they do to achieve that success.* Success over time means success in dealing with change. It means reformation. What does anybody know about this? Would a little knowledge about organizational endurance be helpful to knowing what denominations should do in the twenty-first century? Are there enduring principles that cut across time and that are not so subject to the come and go of management fads?

Three popular efforts are worthy of note. The most well known of these, *In Search of Excellence,* by Thomas Peters and Robert Waterman (1982), has sold over seven million copies. The popularity of the book gives the impression it covers the best of the fads with its emphasis on "eight steps to success." It is a serious attempt, however, to move "toward theory"—that is, to identify conceptual hooks on which to hang one's experience long enough to get one's bearings before plunging back into the swirl of everyday organizational life. One clue to appreciating the book is not to read it as a quick fix, but as an attempt to uncover time-tested principles.

Another attempt at identifying enduring principles is *Built to Last,* by James Collins and Jerry Porras (1994). The question Collins and Porras hoped to answer is why some business firms last while others do not. The authors identified a list of visionary companies lasting more than fifty years, limited it to eighteen, then compared each with a company in the same industry in order to identify the differences between each pair.

A third interesting search for enduring principles is *The Living Company*, by Arie de Geus (1997). De Geus focuses on twenty-seven companies in existence for over one hundred years. The basic premise of the book is that a company is actually a living system that learns in much the same way individuals do.

These three studies—*In Search of Excellence, Built to Last,* and *The Living Company*—are grounded in the study of actual organizations. They are appealing because they exhibit sound research practices; they come to similar but not identical conclusions; they are modest, almost embarrassed by the mundaneness of their findings; they make liberal use of the academic literature; and, most importantly, they provide useful insights into why organizations last a long time. We will cover them briefly.

The Studies in Review
In Search of Excellence

In Search of Excellence describes people at peak performance, doing what they like, fulfilling their dreams. Our paraphrase is: Here is what you should have been doing all along. We have looked at some excellent companies and have learned some lessons from them. We'd like to share these lessons with you. They have mostly to do with human behavior. We're going to cite some of the literature on human behavior, especially motivation, because we believe that it is the most important thing to look at—human needs in the workplace rather than the Rational Model, which counts things. We believe excellent companies deal with meaning and purpose. They manage ambiguity and paradox. They try hard. They "show up." They don't develop a grand scheme and then apply it. Instead, they try something, step back to learn from it, and try it again. They make change incrementally. We believe there is some relationship between eight features of excellent companies and a new theory of organizations or better organizing. Even the book's title suggests that there may be no arriving, only evolving. There is no body of knowledge about excellent companies, only clues that might explain some things. Welcome to the journey. It's a great ride.

Counting things is never enough. The bottom line, in and of itself, is never enough. Organizations need more. People need more. Both the organization and its people need a deeper purpose—a purpose that carries them when things are not obvious. There is never a single, tried and true way of doing things. Instead, people need a way of moving through when they are surrounded by ambiguity and paradox. This way of moving has as much to do with the value of human relationships as anything else—doing things that add value to people's lives. If this deeper purpose exists, then people can be set free to do their work, to be entrepreneurs, to create. Core purposes are what tie people together but simultaneously loosen them up.

Built to Last

A visionary company not only has a core ideology, but it works hard to preserve it. It stimulates progress through a variety of specific means. It is seldom driven by the short run. It knows that either-or thinking is inadequate and works to find the means for achieving "both . . . and." For example, the company is both stable *and* changing; conservative *and* bold; low-cost *and* high-quality; creative *and* autonomous, while being controlled *and* consistent; it is methodical in its planning *and* unafraid of the unknown; it creates wealth *while* adding value; it is idealistic (value-driven) *and* pragmatic (profit-driven); it preserves the core *while* stimulating progress. It has big goals *and* a cult-like culture. It tries a lot of stuff and keeps what works. Its management comes from within. Doing "good" work is never enough.

The Living Company

A company is a living entity, meaning that it has self-perception and an awareness of time. It also must be aware of its environment, which is an indication of its ability to learn and adapt. It has an identity and an ability to build community. It is, at the same time, able to relate well to the outside world. It is fiscally conservative. It has control over its own growth; it is planned and systematic. It evaluates itself well. It values people, not assets. It is interested in shaping the human community.

The Principles in Diagram

A Must	Expressed As	Resulting In
	Actions consistent with the core but which push forward	
Clarity about identity, core values	A constant flow of new ideas and methods	A mission in context: an evolving fit with environment (congruent or countercultural)
	A conservative management of resources	
	Ongoing concern for people and their growth, community building	

The key dynamic is the ability to learn, given the speed of change.

Seven Strengths

Organizations with staying power seem to engage in a dynamic movement that holds identity and mission together in tension. That tension is creative, not destructive, as attention is given to seven important aspects of organizational life: identity, learning, community building, the generation of new ideas, the creation of resources, the ability to understand and adapt to the environment, and actions that push forward toward innovation.

Identity

It may be surprising to learn from these three studies that enduring organizations do not indiscriminately embrace a mission or set of actions designed to meet or satisfy any expressed need. Instead, they embark on projects that are consistent with *basic elements of an enduring identity*. The question is not so much "What is there to do?" but "What should we do as an expression of who we are, given the specific historical and cultural circumstances we are in and are likely to experience in the future?" There is strong evidence to suggest that organizations fail when they act outside their own parameters. The psychologist Robert Jay Lifton claims that individuals deteriorate when their core sense of identity is violated. He calls it "intactness" versus "diffusion" (Lifton, 1976:38). These three studies give credence to a similar claim for organizations.

Pushy Actions

It would be a mistake to conclude that enduring organizations pursue the same activities over time. Quite the contrary, they take on new ideas and actions constantly, but they are never far from the organization's sense of core identity. Organizational literature is resplendent with examples of companies that abandon some heralded project adopted in the name of diversification or alliance building with the admission, "This endeavor was just not us" or "This project took us away from our core competencies." On the other hand, to keep doing the same thing year after year is a denial of the reality of change. Some denominations now ordain women, when previously they did not. Is that a response to a new fad? The denominations would answer no. This change in policy is consistent with who we are *and* a recognition of a fundamental change in the understanding of the role of women. The theological principle on which such decisions are made is not an abandonment of past commitments but rather recognition of the ongoingness of God's way with us. The resurrection of Jesus did not fit into ancient categories; it was God doing a new thing.

A Flow of New Ideas

What fuels actions that push identity forward and keep it fresh? Organizations that last over time develop a tolerance for new ideas; in fact, they create conditions that encourage and attract new ideas on how to do things. A pastor was meeting with a congregation as a part of the call process. A member asked, "Pastor, can you describe a 'grand mistake' you have made in your ministry?" The pastor replied, "A grand mistake? Can you say more about what you mean?" The member explained, "Some new idea you tried that didn't work. I'm looking for a pastor who tries out new things, some of which probably don't work, but were worth a try." While the member and congregation may be unusual, that attitude reflects an understanding of what these studies observe. Organizations don't last because they shield themselves from fresh perspectives; they last precisely because they entertain a constant flow of new possibilities.

Organized for Learning

Closely allied to pushy actions and new ideas is the concept of learning organizations or, more accurately, *organizing for learning*. Much has been written about the learning organization as the only way to contend with the speed of change. The assumption is that, given the limited alternatives available at any particular time, it is unlikely that a "correct" action can be taken very often. What *can* be done is to take the best possible step and, with learning devices in place, learn from that action, improve it, and then try again. Organizing for learning means more than evaluating meetings or events such as church conferences or conventions, although evaluation is always a good thing to do. What seems to be needed is both the designation of staff competent in evaluation concepts and methods, and instilling an attitude of learning. Marshall McLuhan, the communication guru of several decades ago, is described as constantly bothering his colleagues at McGill University with the question, "Well, what did you learn today?" The shortage of funding for infrastructure in denominational national and regional offices works against the development of this strength.

Community Building

Most of the organizations in these studies are for-profit business firms. It may be a surprise, therefore, that these organizations pay attention to people, not just in words but deeds. In fact, the evidence shows that these organizations are active in developing a sense of community among employees and with outside partners such as suppliers, regulators, and customers. Given the tendency for contemporary organizations to treat employees as a commodity to be downsized, cheated out of pension benefits, and even lied to, it is no easy task to create a sense of community. More is needed than holiday parties, retirement receptions, and snappy employee newsletters. The building of community has to do with participation in key decisions and direction setting; setting clear expectations; appropriate, not exorbitant rewards; education in core values; and opportunities for growth and responsibility. An organization is not a family, but it may exhibit some of the positive aspects of family life.

Conservative Finances

The sixth strength operating in the dynamic of holding identity and mission together is the conservative management of resources. This concept is easily misunderstood. It is not about the avoidance of risks or the hoarding of money. Enduring organizations stay in control of their ability to determine their own destiny. Two slogans this strength does *not* employ are "money is no object" or "we can't accomplish anything without more money." The organization that lasts commits its resources but avoids overcommitment or depending on the next big deal to save it. The trend towards outside partnerships and alliances to provide needed income as core business funds is a dangerous course of action. Denominations may be susceptible to a view that "God will provide," thereby undertaking projects without counting the costs.

Mission in Context

The final observation about lasting organizations is that their sense of mission fits the situation at hand. That little word *fit* is a complex idea. Just think of the many ways the Christian community has related to its surrounding culture all the way from a fortress mentality to almost complete assimilation by the world around it. Recent studies in the ways faith relates to culture describe models of dialogue, critique, correlation, advocacy, praxis, and translation. "Our sole reason for being is mission" is a frequent cry of contemporary denominations. It may be that mission needs to be articulated and implemented in ways that are more specific to the situation at hand.

How Do Denominations Stack Up as Organizations?

Our interviews with denominational leaders and administrators asked about these seven endurance factors. We received some candid responses and many examples. Some of the examples are described in chapter 6: "Incidents of Renewal." Here is a summary of what we heard.

1. The potential is there. None of the seven factors is foreign to church concerns and experiences.
2. Church traditions are steeped with relevant ceremony and skill in identity formation. Some of this self-understanding may need to be brought forward and expressed in new and relevant ways, but of all institutions the church is well-prepared to know who we are and how we got this way. Of the examples shared, more related to *identity* than any of the other six endurance factors.
3. Attempts to develop greater awareness of identity are happening in four ways:

- *Planning exercises,* especially strategic rather than tactical, almost always contain an element of identity development. Mission, vision, and identity statements are the usual ways this is done, but sometimes a glimpse back at denominational history is also included.
- *Identity campaigns* for advertising on television, radio, billboards, and in newspapers have been highly creative ways for stating an identity, sometimes in a few words. The Church of the Brethren is a wonderful example: "Continuing the Work of Jesus: Peacefully, Simply, Together" (see chapter 6 for a more complete description).
- *Identity statements* are direct communication tools, more for internal than external use. These statements attempt to address the challenge of differences within the denominational family and try to provide a glue to hold things together.
- *Web sites* have brought a new opportunity for self-definition and self-presentation. Surf the Web for the sites of the denominations named in this book for a creative display of identity understandings, and affirmations.

4. The greatest need may be in the area of organizational learning. Denominational structures do not usually include resources for reflection or evaluation. Busy denominational staff, the expectations of whom have not diminished, contrary to the rhetoric about decline and decay, have little time or receive insignificant encouragement to pause for the sake of learning. Yet this strength of enduring organizations may be the one with the greatest potential for renewal.
5. Openness to new ideas consistent with identity may be hard to achieve in practice. There is sharing of ideas across denominational lines and sharing within denominations. The evidence, however, leads to the conclusion that borrowed ideas do not produce expected results unless they are shaped to fit both identity and mission needs.

6. Conservative management of resources has been forced on denominations in the last two decades as more is "kept at home." However, our interviews show an intentional effort by leaders to manage the money trusted to them in a highly accountable and transparent fashion. This endurance factor is so basic to building trust and credibility within the denomination and in the perception of the public that it must be done well, both technically and by the communication of important information, trends, and needs. Denominational leaders are judged by the way resources are managed.

7. Identifying pushy ideas did not come easily for most interviewed. We speculate that this is the case for two reasons. What denominations are doing has not been characterized as pushy. Yet after reflection, some things could be described as pushy, such as studies of policy related to homosexuality, new styles of mission development both in the United States and around the world, advocacy work with the government, and evangelism emphases. One example is the Episcopal Church's new plan to build on the theme, "Building a church of disciples who make disciples."

Second, denominations are caught up in the liberal-versus-conservative struggle. One of the themes we are promoting is that the future of denominations has to do with the ability to strengthen the seven factors identified above, which in turn may circumscribe the warfare within. If one has been reading the e-mail and snail-mail responses to a particular aspect of that warfare, one may not be inclined to push or risk anything. But if the theory holds, pushy ideas are a key to endurance.

8. The interviews conducted and materials reviewed about mission-in-context reveal that much effort has gone into formal planning processes with minimal results. There are two kinds of exceptions. When planning leads to initiatives, directions, affirmations, or imperatives linked to budget development, *then* planning is seen as worthwhile. A second exception is when mission planning helps new leaders in self-definition and the building of credibility.

What Are the Prospects?

Viewed through the lens of organizations, especially enduring ones, the future of denominations stacks up rather well. People who lead denominations are not chosen for their organizational skills. However, there is sufficient awareness among those leaders and a willingness to call on church members, staff, and consultants to pay attention to the seven strengths of endurance described in this chapter.

In addition, three of the seven—identity, mission-centered focus, and community building—are naturals for denominations. This means they are already present in the theology, history, tradition, and ministries. These three may need tweaking a bit or revitalization, but they are there to be called upon. The other four—pushy actions, flow of new ideas, organizational learning, and conservative finances—present challenges to denominations. But if this interpretation of organizational endurance contains some truth, then these are also potential growth areas for denominations and warrant increased attention and work.

6. INCIDENTS OF RENEWAL

The fashioning of new patterns of [church] organizational life from whatever materials are at hand will require a great deal of imagination, care and even courage.
— Craig Dystra and James Hudnut-Beumler, 1991

A re there any detectable signs of life in contemporary denominations? Or have they rolled over, waiting for the inevitable end? This chapter lifts up nine kinds of activities that seem to us examples worth noticing. We move through them quickly. Much more could be said, but we want to provide a sense of the scope and variety of activities. All of which show the commitment of mainline denominations to forming and strengthening community. These activities are responses to life in contemporary American society that are born neither of denial nor despair, but out of a dogged commitment to keep working in difficult and complex circumstances. These efforts bear the marks of both reality (what is) and possibility (what could be). We take them as signs of hope. They are incidents of renewal. They show mainline denominations always asking more of themselves and the wider society. They show the discontent of mainline denominations with quick and easy answers and with isolation and individualism.

1. Identity: Roots and Self-Understanding

The pressures of being and doing church have not only driven denominations to look forward into a daunting future, but also backward and inward in search of greater clarity on identity. We have made much of the need for community and the importance of mainline denominations as a means of achieving it. Like individuals, denominations have an identity. Earlier in this book we called on Eric Erikson. He posited that identity involves three dynamics: the more durable features of personality over time, an engagement of the issues and needs of the times, and an attempt at self-cure. We believe these dynamics of personal identity can also be attributed to mainline denominations. There is something durable that serves as a guide for mainline denominations wrestling with the issues and needs of the times. Knowing these durable features brings with it the possibility of a cure for the ills that afflict them. For this reason, mainline denominations have taken on a host of significant activities designed to regularly engage the questions of "Who are we?" and "What does it mean?" Notice the emphasis in these examples on living in community.

Church of the Brethren: Distinctive Not Competitive

In 1994, a 66-page report was issued by a group of professional communication consultants to the Church of the Brethren's General Board with four main points: a centuries-old tradition stands in contrast, not in competition with other denominations; the distinctiveness is not in abstract doctrine but in living; there is a denominational pattern of daily living around the humble service of Jesus; and the potential exists to be a compassionate alternative in a world of complexity, alienation, and violence. Theologians and marketing experts put their talents together to conduct focus groups in congregations, prepare Bible studies, and develop "identity lines" for wide use in evangelism, publishing, and planning.

The Church of the Brethren looked back to look forward. What is the Church of the Brethren that the world needs now? It is a church about "replenishment," which is a new way to express an idea that has always been part of the Brethren's core identity. Who are the Brethren? Their motto is:

Another way of living.
Continuing the work of Jesus.
Peacefully.
Simply.
Together.

The Moravian Church in America: Core Values and Bedrock Beliefs

Sometimes called the Moravian motto—"in essentials, unity; in nonessentials, liberty; and in all things charity (or love)"—these words are well known across denominations as a Moravian mark of identity. Less well known is the work of this church's Southern Province to describe "core values" and "bedrock beliefs" as a means of self-understanding. Leaders were gathered during the winter of 2001–2002 to identify actual, not idealized, values that were foundational to the life of the Province. They produced two lists—one of "positive" and one of "negative" core values. The positive core values include: (1) a theology that is Christ-centered and biblically grounded; (2) a heritage that is a legacy to be retooled; (3) a commitment to helping and caring; (4) providing service to members; (5) being generous; and (6) being nonjudgmental as a way of giving witness to the wideness of God's mercy.

The negative core values include: (1) a penchant for stability and a tendency to maintain a rather narrow understanding of the tradition; (2) a commitment to institutional preservation and an inward orientation; (3) an overt congregationalism putting a high value on local autonomy.

According to Robert E. Hunter, Assistant to the President, Southern Province, the "bedrock beliefs" were easier for the leaders to describe. He notes that these bedrock beliefs are "often most evident when we examine what maintains us in times of crisis." The bedrock beliefs include the following: (1) God, who is the creator and sovereign of all the universe, is always present with us; (2) God loves us; (3) God calls us into a community of faith in Jesus Christ; (4) Christ, and him crucified, shall remain the confession of faith; (5) Christ's resurrection is God's victory over death and the assurance that in Christ we have new life; (6) Jesus is our Savior, companion, and Lord of our lives; and (7) God calls us to live out the sacrificial love of Christ and serve the world that God loves and redeems.

Christian Reformed Church in North America: Three Churches or One?

Like many denominations, the Christian Reformed Church finds itself facing an increasing divergence of styles in belief and practice. In a remarkable "head on" approach, they have identified three different ways of being Reformed. The goal was to affirm them all as a source for unity and cohesion while identifying their similarities and differences. The three approaches to being Reformed include: (1) a Doctrinalist emphasis that primarily understands being reformed in terms of beliefs; (2) a Pietist emphasis that places its focus on how God is experienced in the daily walk of faith; and (3) a Transformationalist emphasis that places its primary attention on how the gospel relates to the world.

Peter Borgdorff, Executive Director of Ministries, recounts how looking forward (through strategic planning) called forth the need to look backward at the denomination's history. The strategic plan was dependent upon citing the identity of the church which, in turn, consists of the values and principles that have guided the church "along the way."

Is the Christian Reformed Church one church or three? The answer: one church affirming the role and place of all three emphases within Christian life and the Christian Church. Lutheran theologian Joseph Sittler once observed that the Church had experienced a melancholy number of ways to fragment and scatter; what is needed in obedience to Christ are creative ways to unite and gather (Sittler, 1962:14). The identity statement of the Christian Reformed Church is a prime example of seeking out the latter.

The Reformed Church in America: An Identity Event

June 9–15, 2000, was the occasion for this denomination to name elements of identity and mission in a creative way. A convocation was held in New York City called Mission 2000. The convocation itself was part of a three-phase approach: (1) praying and preparing; (2) gathering and discussing; and (3) engaging the world by following Christ. Forty-six discernment groups met during the convocation for in-depth reflection and interaction.

Why New York City? That is where the Reformed Church began. The Reformed Church in America has its historical roots in the New Amsterdam in 1623 when the Reformed Church in the Netherlands sent a pastor to serve a congregation of fifty members. The famous Collegiate Churches of New York City are an example of their early work. A historical walk of sites important in the history of the denomination along with a variety of Discovery Groups were offered. The annual General Synod met within the larger convocation. The goal was to combine legislative sessions with time for celebration, remembering, discernment, planning, and education. Legislation often divides, but celebrating and remembering brings people together. It affirms and reaffirms the community.

United Church of Christ: Firsts

The Web site of the United Church of Christ has many of the same features as other denominational Web sites. It lists officers, the history of the church, its structure, characteristics, beliefs, and current events. One feature, however, stands out. A list of "firsts" is described as the United Church of Christ remembers its marks on religion in the Untied States. Here is a sample of the "firsts" among the twenty-one offered. Think of the community-building aspects of reflecting on these firsts as the United Church of Christ works toward the ideal of an American community.

1700. An early stand against slavery.
1773. First published African American poet.
1777. Salvaging the Liberty Bell by hiding it under a church.
1785. First ordination of an African American pastor.
1840. First United Church in U.S. history.
1853. First woman pastor.
1943. The "Serenity Prayer" (theologian Reinhold Niebuhr).
1959. Historic ruling that airwaves are public property.
1972. First ordination of an openly gay minister.
1976. First African American leader of a mainline denomination.

Edith A. Guffey, Associate General Minister, calls these "firsts" examples that "God is still speaking." They are also evidence of how a denomination can define its identity both within and to the wider public. It is a powerful way to build identity that distinguishes itself from using only doctrine or ecclesiology.

2. Dialogue and Relationship Building

As with identity, mainline denominations are seeking new ways to bridge the divide, both among the various expressions of their churches and among their members. One way to close the gap is through intentional dialogue. On the difficult issues that separate people in the wider society, it is probably true that the differences within any particular mainline denomination are greater than those between them. It is both a liability and a wonderful asset to have members with different points of view. After all, there is ground to build upon. They still call themselves Methodists, Presbyterians, or Lutherans.

The models we quickly review below are designed not only to promote civil discourse but also to create new arenas where members can engage each other in significant ways as part of a community. When official, legislative discussions are held, normally according to Roberts Rules of Order, tough decisions are made by vote (majority, two-thirds, etc.). In this context, depth of understanding and a positive experience of community are often sacrificed. It is true that many people become impatient and want to make "the decision" and move on, but perhaps mainline denominations should be slow about finalizing things by voting. Perhaps patience should be their mark. Mainline denominations are sometimes accused of being behind the times. We think it is more accurate to say that they are slow, sometimes not slow enough, to decide. There should be a genuine search for dialogue within mainline denominations. The words of 1 Peter 4:8-10 for building up Christian community come to mind: "Above all keep fervent in your love for one another, because love covers a multitude of sins. Be hospitable to one another without complaint. As each has received a special gift, employ it in serving one another as good stewards of the manifold grace of God."

American Baptist Churches USA: Adopting New Models for Dialogue

Bringing people together from diverse backgrounds and points of view is a part of the primary role of mainline denominations. Knowing how to "talk to each other" and providing a set of guidelines for doing so are crucial to fulfilling their role. The American Baptist Churches USA have adopted two models to assist them in dealing with difficult issues that could potentially divide. The first model seeks "Common Ground." In the very description of the principles of Common Ground, it is possible to gain a sense of how it works: (1) Common Ground creates interlocking circles; (2) Common Ground honors each individual's piece of the truth; (3) Common Ground is about "shedding light, not creating heat;" (4) Common Ground is not compromise; (5) Common Ground recognizes a continuum of perceptions.

The second model is the Principled Negotiation Model drawn from the Harvard Negotiation Project. It has been used among American Baptist executives to develop new budget covenants and changes in national programs and structure. There are four principles to the model: (1) separate people from the problem; (2) focus on interests, not positions; (3) invent options for mutual gain; and (4) insist on criteria.

The United Methodist Church: Help from John Wesley

Sometimes, in promoting dialogue, the oldest is as valuable as the newest technique. The United Methodist Church mission statement contains the phrase, "We will strive for deeper relationships." Several commissions have provided guidelines and developed opportunities for Methodists to dialogue over matters of faith, mission, and church. One recent effort called "The Search for Unity" involves the use of dialogue techniques as well as liturgical resources, including two sermons by John Wesley. These sermons are the "Catholic Spirit" and "On Schism." They are primary examples of how an informed use of the past can be of invaluable service to the future.

Presbyterian Church (USA): Tending to Relationships

Relationships need tending. Even when a strong foundation has been laid, attention has to be paid to maintaining relationships. In the Presbyterian church, a presbytery is the corporate expression of the church within a certain district. It consists of elders and ministers. The Presbyterian Church (USA) has 176 presbyteries divided into nineteen synods. The Book of Order describes functions and relationships. A monumental effort is underway to visit synods and presbyteries by the Stated Clerk, Cliff Kirpatick, and the Executive Director of the General Assembly Council, John B. Deterrich. When these two leaders meet with the synods and presbyteries, they ask, "What is God doing here in this place?" Kathy McMullen Lueckert, Deputy Executive Director, describes these visits as "a positive force" in denominational life. Community is based on clarity in speaking and hearing, and given the powerful forces working against clarity, church officials have to go "out of their way."

The Presbyterians have also been working on a paper entitled "Only Together. Conversations About Partnership. A Work in Progress." The paper provides an opportunity to confess past failures at partnership; to ground partnership in Christian community; to describe the necessity of partnerships in a world of rapid change; to identify the values that undergird and mark healthy partnerships; and to project the hopes, principles, behavior, and expectations for partnerships. One challenge to partnership is the question: "How do you get everyone in on the action and still get some action?" The paper provides some practical answers. "When partnership is used to define the style in which the church intends to work, it implies flexibility and openness to change, a church always being reformed 'according to the Word of God and the call of the Spirit'" *(Book of Order)*. Tending to relationships and actually getting something done is a tension that goes to the very core of mainline denominations and, as a result, it is a tension that needs to be embraced rather than erased.

Evangelical Lutheran Church in America: Tending to Relationships

As the Evangelical Lutheran Church in America emerged from its early years after merger in 1988, something was needed to keep the sixty-five synods and the national (churchwide) office in touch, as well as each synod with its congregations. Annual meetings called "consultations" met the need. Focused conversations on mission, context, issues, partnership, and funding have provided an important addition to the regular contacts among church leaders.

Four kinds of consultations have occurred on a rotating basis so that each synod can be involved each year with a small team of national staff. These consultations range from a simple telephone call; to a meeting of national representatives with entire synod councils; to a region or sub-region meetings of representatives of each synod including one bishop from another region in addition to members of the national church council; to a three-day on-site visit of national representatives with a synod council, groups of pastors, congregational members, and representatives of agencies or institutions affiliated with the church. Ongoing evaluation keeps the consultations fresh and provides the input for agenda development. Church structures need to be supplemented and complemented with innovative ways to enhance communication and build relationships for the sake of community.

Synergies

It is important to note in passing that the need for community and a means for dialogue that builds rather than destroys is so great that other, nonovertly religious institutions are also regularly experimenting, testing, and employing new community-building strategies for their own ends. As a result, an interesting, ever-evolving set of tools for dialogue is available to mainline denominations. We noted above how the American Baptists have made use of some of these tools. Perhaps mainline denominations should be more intentional about giving back, both to each other and to the wider set of interested institutions. Maybe the Methodists should consider, for example, letting the world in on the power of John Wesley's sermons. Luther had a word or two to say about freedom and restraint in the search of community as well. And then, of course, there are the more direct lessons from the New Testament.

As it is, a synergy of sharing, often unexamined, is already taking place. For example, it does not take long to see that the "learning organization" from business and government circles has adopted religious principles and, in turn, mainline denominations have borrowed techniques developed from the best in this new "learning organization" movement. Modern organizations of all kinds want to learn quickly and deeply so they can better cope with the speed of change. Peter Senge (1990:238) (based on the conceptual work of David Bohm) calls for establishing conditions for dialogue inside organizations so that learning happens in quicker cycles than in the past. How can this be achieved? It can only be achieved through high levels of commitment to a community of trust and caring. In fact, the entire "total quality" movement is about individuals in community.

In this same vein, another approach to community building can be traced to the philosopher Martin Buber (1958) (I-Thou relationships differ from I-It relationships). Buber's ideas have had a significant impact on modern education and in governmental settings. The synergy is around every turn. Take a look, for example, at pollster Daniel Yankelovich's *The Magic of Dialogue* (1999). Yankelovich, describing the "magic" of dialogue, offers an abundance of ideas and tools for collaborative and participatory conversation that leads to common understanding and action. It is also worth pointing out that the entire discussion on postmodernism in the field of philosophy, including its positing of the loss of a "grand narrative" to hold things together, has launched an investigation into the very nature of discourse. Where there is a paucity of shared values and commitments, how do we carry on a conversation that moves beyond tribalism, regionalism, and "we-they" to understanding, appreciation, and even common action? For at least the last decade, many mainline denominations have taken on the challenge of equipping their members to engage each other in a civil manner over tough issues about which there is widespread disagreement. They have undertaken these activities in a very difficult environment and often at their own peril but with the consistent hope for community. Mainline denominations should more conscientiously contribute to the synergy in the wider society that has as its goal building relationships and strengthening community.

3. Forming Alliances

As society takes on the appearance and reality of a web, that is, a networked set of independent entities, denominations are also forming new configurations of cooperation and mutual support. Again, with theories and practices borrowed from the public, private, and social sectors, denominations are forming new ways of working that honor autonomy, yet create cooperative strategies that benefit all the participants. There is something other than disconnected, even alienated institutions "doing their own thing" on the one hand, and total uniformity and lock-step obedience on the other. Finding that "something" can get us past the pendulum swings from centralization to decentralization and back again by pursuing both in appropriate measure. The potential of these kinds of alliances is exciting. They illustrate how "old" denominational patterns can move into new ways of thinking and doing. Creating alliances is a means for creating community.

Evangelical Lutheran Church in America: Alliance Building

For five years, a group of twelve to twenty ELCA churchwide staff met for half a day about four times a year around the topic of strengthening external relationships. Discussing literature about alliances and their own experiences, they presented "case studies" to each other and eventually constructed a theory of alliance-building to evaluate these experiences. The theory covered objectives, partners, the nature of relationships, and long- and short-term outcomes. Several "axioms" emerged. Alliances involve gains and losses, but they seldom achieve a balance. Put differently, alliances often mean giving as much as getting, and in that context the "risks" of alliances can be managed, but never eliminated. Challenges were also clarified. Seeking the appropriate autonomy for partners and appropriate coordination is essential to creating "one system." Finding and developing new competencies needed to build alliances is often neglected but absolutely necessary.

This denomination has two examples of alliance-building that are alive and well. Lutheran Services in America is an alliance of 280 Lutheran social ministry organizations in 3,000 locations officially organized on April 13, 1997. It is a joint effort of the ELCA and the Lutheran Church–Missouri Synod. This arrangement provides the benefits of an alliance while allowing and encouraging the freedom of individual organizations to fulfill their purposes in their local and regional locations. Linkages to the two denominations are also established so that while the alliance is "outside" the denominational structure, it does not operate autonomously. The purpose of the alliance is to "support the Lutheran Church to extend the love of Christ through ministries of service and justice" as the member organizations "work together on the strategic issues."

The second example is the result of a theological education study recommended in 1993 and 1995, that the eight ELCA-affiliated seminaries come together to form a "single system." At a time when the prevailing organizational wisdom emphasized decentralization, such an alliance was counter-intuitive. Many believed that the seminaries should be cut loose to attract students, funding, and supporters to the best of their abilities. The results of the study, however, created "one theological system," "three clusters," and "eleven imperatives" common to all eight seminaries.

One key seemed to be the development of intermediate means for shared commitment such as business plans and cooperative programs (e.g., Doctor of Ministry and distance education). Efforts that are highly collaborative in nature sometimes falter because they cannot find a middle ground. These efforts end up overrelying on general slogans or go too deep in developing detailed procedures that lead to fatigue instead of collaboration. The alliance of ELCA seminaries creates something in between that is sustaining common efforts for the benefit of all over the long run.

Christian Church (Disciples of Christ) and the United Church of Christ: A Global Ministries Alliance

These two denominations do global mission together through cooperative work in selected mission fields. From a conversation that started in 1965 to a Common Global Ministries Board in 1996, planning, budgeting, and field work are now carried out jointly. This alliance, called an "ecumenical partnership," is described as "a common witness" of the Division of Overseas Ministries of the Disciples of Christ and the Wider Church Ministries of the United Church of Christ.

The mission statement commits each denomination to "a shared life in Christ" and to "an ecumenical global sharing of resources and prophetic vision of a just and peaceful world order." Theirs is not a merger; it is an expression of "covenantal bonds." One of the guiding principles reads, "recognizing the freedom of God's spirit to act in diverse ways, we commit ourselves to engage in dialogue, witness and common cause with people of other faiths and movements with whom we share a vision of peace, justice and integrity of creation."

4. Outreach and Evangelism

Much has been written about the growth and decline of the membership of mainline denominations and we add to the commentary in chapter 4 of this book. No matter what the odds against turnaround growth, almost every mainline denomination has an evangelism strategy of one sort or another. A lot is known about what works and doesn't work with regard to evangelism. Some very well conceived and executed endeavors have produced positive short-term results, only to suffer a decline (at least numerically) akin to the decline associated with the development, introduction, and maturity of "products" in the business sector. There is much inertia and even cynicism about the capacity of denominations to "reach out," especially to groups that are ethnically, culturally, or economically different from themselves. "So, what shall we do?" is the question. How do mainline denominations that shy away from strict and literal theological doctrinal formulations, with members that are unlikely to argue publicly even among friends for the preeminence of their doctrinal beliefs, ever go out and attempt to convince others that religious faith can make a difference in their lives. In chapter 4 we suggest that strictness about doctrinal beliefs is not the only alternative. We encourage mainline denominations to focus on their commitment to community. In this way, mainline denominations can reach out and "witness," based not on the fear of being "left behind" but in a very positive response to God's graciousness in our own lives.

The Episcopal Church in the United States of America: Making Disciples

Few people seem to know that the incorporated name of the Episcopal Church is "The Domestic and Foreign Missionary Society of the Protestant Episcopal Church in the United States." Surprised? The name is a reminder of the origins of many mainlines, namely independent "societies" which eventually were brought together in a "loose-tight" set of arrangements depending on a certain shared ethos and set of beliefs. But, the name also illustrates how the missionary imperative both at home and abroad was near the heart of why denominations were created in the first place.

We should not be surprised, then, to find the Episcopal Church developing a bold new evangelism strategy titled "Doubling by 2020: Building a church of disciples who make disciples." The Episcopal Church has a dream.

> It is our dream that when 2020 arrives, as many as 25 percent of our congregations will be less than 20 years old and that, the percentage of our worshiping members will have doubled from the present 830,000 each Sunday, and the median age of our parishes will be considerably younger. It is also our fervent hope that those who are Episcopalian in 2020 will socially and ethnically "look more like America" as a whole than we do today.

The report of the 2020 task force addresses leadership, generations, Hispanic ministry, budgets, history, accountability, demographics, research, spirituality, and vision. It calls for funding training of a youth minister in each congregation and a ministry on college campuses; expanded leadership training for those under thirty-five to include internships, mentoring, service projects and multicultural experiences, and contemporary second language training; moving toward debt free education for clergy vocations; and moving toward seeking entrepreneurs and risk-takers among the brightest and best for ordained ministry. Finally, the strategy challenges the church to create contemporary liturgies, music and prayers that fit "today's culture" and for planting new churches.

Evangelical Lutheran Church in America: Sharing Faith in A New Century

At the 2003 Churchwide Assembly of the Evangelical Lutheran Church in America, a new evangelism strategy was approved called "Sharing Faith in a New Century." The strategy is based in a commitment to change the reserved, circumspect, and parochial tendencies of the members and congregations of the church. It seeks to reaffirm the ELCA's commitment to both the biblical mandate to "Go, therefore, and make disciples" (Matt. 28:19-20), and the church's constitutional charge to participate in God's mission by proclaiming "God's saving Gospel of justification by grace for Christ's sake through faith alone."

The strategy sets out four basic goals:

1. to activate and mobilize the church to pray for renewal that is grounded in the Word
2. to prepare and renew evangelical leaders, lay and clergy, by reaffirming evangelism as a key priority
3. to teach people of all ages to live as disciples of Jesus Christ, sent as witnesses to Jesus, in service to others and working for justice and peace in all the world
4. to increase the number of ELCA congregations and ministry sites, which are growing spiritually and numerically

The Lutheran Church–Missouri Synod: Plan B?

This denomination is one of those that grew quickly from 1850 into the 1900s primarily through Northern European immigration. America was very attractive to German Lutherans looking for a better life. But, the Northern European influx is over. Charles S. Mueller (with Wheat Ridge Ministries) asks his church, "Do we have a Plan B?" Mueller suggests something different than simply another evangelism program. It is unlikely that the Germans disembarking from the boats in the late 1800s asked about the location of the nearest Lutheran church. Rather, they were "evangelized" by those who met the boats in New Orleans, New York, and Baltimore. And, those German immigrants were not all alike. Some were fleeing religious persecution. Others were draft dodgers. Others were tired of Europe and wanted new opportunities, and some were running from religion itself. The point is that within the tradition of the Lutheran Church–Missouri Synod, the ability to reach out to people with different wants and needs has already shown itself. If it was done once, maybe it can happen again. The past can be brought forward, to spark new ways of seeing and doing.

Bradford Hewitt, former Executive Director of the Board of Directors for the Lutheran Church–Missouri Synod, points out that from the beginning, the church had two challenges. The first was the desire for a way to differentiate itself from the more accommodating state churches of Europe. The second was how to attract new members in the new land. These old challenges have evolved into a "new demand" which "is to tell the story," according to Hewitt, "in a way that is attractive in a pluralistic age while being faithful to the gospel."

Many members of mainline churches, especially those who appealed to European immigrants, tend to feel that reaching out to people with other ethnic heritages is an impossible dream. At its worst, it is a kind of demand that makes people feel inadequate because of past failures or a sense that one needs to abandon the tradition in a rush toward something new and unrecognizable. The Lutheran Church–Missouri Synod has noticed that within their history is the encouragement and perhaps the confidence to reach out. The logic is, "We did it before. We can do it again."

The United Methodist Church: Igniting Ministry

92 million people reached.

25,000 church leaders trained.

Worship attendance up.

What's this? Signs of resignation in a dying church? The United Methodists offer these results from an imaginative use of media combined with the engagement of local churches to welcome those whose interest has been sparked by the media. Igniting Ministry has three goals: (1) to increase awareness and recognition of the United Methodist Church's basic beliefs; (2) to foster among nonmembers a positive feeling and willingness to visit a United Methodist church; and (3) to renew a sense of commitment among United Methodists. A five point program is underway.

- Seventeen TV ads, 40 radio ads, over 300 pieces of print advertising;
- Distributing more than 13,000 planning kits to local churches;

- Training 25,000 local church leaders;
- Providing $1 million in matching grants to local churches and conferences;
- Setting up a Web site to help seekers learn more about the United Methodist Church or to locate a local church.

Approval is being sought to post an electronic billboard in Times Square in New York City using the "Open Hearts, Open Minds, Open Doors" theme. This theme is explained as "caring hearts for those in need, open-mindedness that requires no commitment to a mandatory creed, and open doors to people with diverse opinions, cultural traditions, and ethnic backgrounds and beliefs" (from a brochure of the campaign).

Public awareness of the media component of the campaign is tracked by research. Afraid to evaluate? Not this program. Rev. Steve Horswill-Johnston, staff person responsible for program development, reports that awareness of the United Methodist Church in test markets has increased to 21 percent in the first two years. Also 46 percent of nonmembers surveyed expressed a willingness to attend a Methodist church, which is a 10 percent increase over the goal (United Methodist Church press release for July 18, 2003).[1]

Igniting Ministry is not a quick fix. The long-term commitment of the United Methodist Church is found in a request to the 2004 General Conference to increase the 2005–2008 budget from $20 million to $33.5 million and to fund a new youth version with $5.4 million. Rev. Larry Hallon, chief staff executive of the United Methodist Church's Communication Commission, says the United Methodist Church "has delivered messages of hope at critical times in recent history and has extended an invitation to Christian community . . . through Igniting Ministry" (United Methodist Church press release for July 18, 2003).

In the early days of the Republic, itinerant Methodist preachers known as circuit riders brought the gospel to those on the frontier often at personal peril and hardship. During these early years of the twenty-first century, the same daring, imagination, and commitment is alive in the newest of the United Methodist Church's endeavors to present the gospel with power using the new technology of the media age in which the mainline denominations operate today.

5. Structural Revision and Adjustment

It seems to have happened so often over the last few decades that no one is surprised. The church is restructuring again. "It is like rearranging the deck chairs on the *Titanic*." While some restructuring is an avoidance of real problems and issues, there is a genuine search for forms that support mission and ministry for the next century. The importance of structure is probably both over- and underestimated. Restructuring takes time, skill, and money. Fadism abounds. Does having the "right" structure, that is, one appropriate to the organization's mission, vision, values, and resources, make any real difference? Won't just any structure do? After all, the common wisdom is that people make the structure work, so why bother about structure at all? In terms of this chapter, why is tinkering with structure a sign of renewal?

There is a growing body of evidence, the description of which is beyond the purpose of this book, that structure is more significant than previously thought. Over the last two years, newspaper reports have tracked the affairs of the United States Olympic Committee.[2] On the advice of business consultants, the top governing body of the Olympic movement in the United States installed a board and officials following a corporate model. After all, many people believe the business world is the best place to look for how to run an organization. From time to time, even government leaders have tried to make government run "like a business." And, nonprofits have, on occasion, strayed into the profit world for aid and wisdom. Never mind that the grandfather of modern management, Peter Drucker (Munson, 1989; Juneau and Maglitta, 1991), regularly recommended nonprofits as examples of excellence to profit-making leaders, even devoting his foundation to nonprofit organization learning. But the Olympic movement is not a business. It has a blend of professional and volunteer leadership, gathers financial support from the public, and solicits support from the government. It doesn't need a corporate structure and is now shedding it with great pain and embarrassment especially over power struggles and inflated salaries and benefits for its leaders. It is the same for a denomination. When a denomination grows its structure, that is, creates one expressive of its identity, history, mission, values, and vision of the future, then good things happen. A look at several restructuring projects shows not so much an avoidance of real challenges as faithful attempts to remove obstacles to effectiveness.

Within the last decade, mainline denominations have been restructuring their national offices at a furious rate. If the mainline denominations would work more on the seven strengths detailed in chapter 5: "Built to Last," perhaps they could devote less time to restructuring. "Organized for Learning" is the weakest of the seven strengths based on our review of denominational literature and interviews. Creating a culture of continuing learning, in turn, produces small, incremental corrections and improvements. One way to facilitate continual learning is to rely on "program evaluation" of major program areas to provide information about appropriate corrections. Restructuring, on the other hand, usually results from the need to deal with accumulated problems. If these problems were addressed along the way, then there is less pressure to restructure. One example is the adjustments made by the ELCA in 1991, only two years after its birth. Some of the political compromises necessary to bring about the merger of three Lutheran denominations proved to be unworkable and too expensive. Two major consolidations of program units, converting program boards into advisory committees, and a greater leadership role for the Office of the Bishop "adjusted" the structure without the turmoil and the costs of a comprehensive restructuring.

Another step that can be taken to avoid restructuring is to create teams and work groups that have the ability to cross the intradenominational agency divide. It can often take years to address the constitutional hurdles that confront most reorganizations, but teams can be created as an alternative to constitutional changes. The teams can be used as a means for improving communication and cooperation. They can provide flexibility and can be more easily created and dissolved as needs evolve. And, new technologies make it ever-more possible to create and use virtual teams. Finally, alliances are an alternative to restructuring. Alliances can take on some of the features of more permanent structures while remaining flexible. Again, in the ELCA, two examples are Lutheran Services in America and the theological education system.

The United Church of Christ: Pulling Together Semiautonomous Institutions into a Coherent Whole

It took over a decade, but it was worth it. Edith Guffey, Associate General Minister, says, "Our restructuring has been a confidence builder. It showed we could pull together semiautonomous institutions into a coherent whole and organize them around UCC values and theology." The UCC moved from two large boards (Homeland and International Ministries), nine affiliated instrumentalities (e.g., Women, Racial Justice), and three executive offices, into: two coordinating bodies (Collegium of Officers and Mission Planning Committee), four ministries (Wider Church, Justice and Witness, Local Church, Office of General Ministries and President), and two associated ministries (pensions and foundation). The reorganization was designed to address effectiveness in multicultural ministry, strengthening the Office of General Minister and President, removing overlapping functions as seen from the local church, and reorienting the denomination toward serving local churches.

Evangelical Lutheran Church in America: More Coherence

Coming off a merger of three Lutheran denominations in 1988, the Evangelical Lutheran Church in America was forced to redo its national structure in a short two years. Two principles were important in rethinking what was needed. First, the major work of the churchwide office should be apparent in the names of the units. This was called the communication principle. The second principle emerged from research on members' perceptions of the national office, namely that it was too diffuse, "spread out," "all over the place," "too much" with "too many separate units." The goal, therefore, was to clearly differentiate (the second principle) with regard to their purpose and function. The result was the 6-2-3 design: six divisions, within which the broad and ongoing priorities of the church are clearly embodied, including support for congregational life, domestic outreach ministries, global mission, work in higher education and schools, leadership development and support, and work for service and justice; two commissions, which give structural embodiment to two specific and urgent tasks in the ELCA—to implement the church's commitment to the full participation of persons of color or language other than English and women; and three offices, which support the work of the Presiding Bishop, the Secretary, and the Treasurer.

Advice on Restructuring

When done well, structure should flow from the identity, vision, and values of a denomination, and enable it to do its mission in an ever-changing environment. If, or should we say when, restructuring occurs, it is important to keep the following five points in mind.

1. Denominations can, and should, tap into the experience of people who do organizational design work for a living. One such group is the Organization Design Forum (formerly the Association for the Management of Organizational Design).[3] Many of these professionals are members of mainline denominations.

2. There is much to be learned from other church bodies. Unfortunately, little is actually written down (particularly of a reflective nature), but the rewards of interviewing those with experience may be considerable.

3. It is easy to lose sight of an appropriate balance between centralization and decentralization. Any proposal made that emphasizes one to the exclusion of the other will inevitably cause problems which, in turn, will demand new "adjustments." Almost every recent restructuring of a mainline is an attempt to convert an overzealous decentralization of major functions.

4. It is important to pay attention to the human resource issues early in the process. By whatever name—mergers, consolidations, or the creation of something new—structuring is a fascinating human endeavor. It is fraught with potential for both good and bad. Structuring often presents theological, psychological, organizational, and political challenges. But, most of all, restructuring in particular, presents the ethical challenge of dealing justly with dedicated human beings.
5. Finally, hold something back. Implement a new structure in stages. This strategy allows for midcourse corrections based on learning.

Very soon, the organizations of national offices (and perhaps regional agencies too) may be more virtual ("click") and less physical ("mortar"). Perhaps even the physical necessity of a central office will diminish. In the future, a new "organizational architecture" will emerge tied more to agreed-upon purposes than physical space. We think this may be very exciting and call for a kind of thinking not yet imagined. At the same time, we are not at all sure about what this means to our conception of a community of people working and living together. "Gathering" together may take new forms, which may well call for new "structures." Is it possible to have a "virtual" church?

6. The Poor—Our Teachers

The number of denominations attempting to address ministry with and among the poor is increasing. "Attempt" is the term of choice because their efforts, though sincere, are awkward. They usually have three features: confession, study, and action. Confession involves a recognition of past neglect and attitudes of privilege and superiority. Through study, an attempt is made to understand the sources and effects of poverty and relevant biblical and theological perspectives. Action includes funding for activities addressing domestic and international needs and attitudinal change.

Evangelical Lutheran Church in America: Confession and Funding

The interviews with denominational leaders showed that most of the ministries that have to do with the poor are conducted with social ministry organizations; global mission efforts; fund-raising for world hunger; and development and advocacy work. Two denominations have made special efforts to strengthen their ministry in these areas.

Beginning with a sermon of confession by its then Presiding Bishop, H. George Anderson, to the other Lutheran bishops, the Evangelical Lutheran Church in America asked its churchwide units and agencies, in cooperation with the synods, to identify domestic and international projects and plan new ones. New funding was also provided. In his sermon, Bishop Anderson used the phrase "the poor are our teachers." This key phrase became a new way to understand a community that gives special attention to its relationship with the "least of these."

The United Methodist Church: Bishops' Initiative

In 1996, the Council of Bishops recommended to all congregations the implementation of a response around the growing plight of children in American society. This *Initiative on Children and Poverty*[4] has three goals:

1. To reshape The United Methodist Church in response to the God who is among "the least of these" and the evaluation of everything the church is and does in the light of the impact on children and the impoverished.
2. To provide resources for understanding the crisis among children and the impoverished and enabling the church to respond.
3. To engage in evangelization: the proclamation in word and deed of the gospel of God's redeeming, reconciling, and transforming grace in Jesus Christ to and with children and those oppressed by poverty.

In 2004, the Bishops published the latest "foundation paper" in an effort to help teach the church. The paper is entitled "Our Shared Dream: The Beloved Community." Given our theme of the importance of community in the life of mainline denominations, we quote extensively from the paper's introduction.[5]

> We believe that a vision of the church and of all people as the Beloved Community offers a strong theological framework for the advancement of the Initiative on Children and Poverty and its primary goal: "the reshaping of The United Methodist Church in response to the God who is among 'the least of these.'" We desire to be an expression of the Beloved Community in our life together, "a sign of hope . . . that division, destitution, despair and death [are] being overcome" by the love of God shown in deeds of Jesus—such as living. We recognize that much remains to be done to clarify the relationship between sound doctrine and a commitment to community with the vulnerable and the violated. We are holding before ourselves, and the whole church, a compelling

vision of community with children and the poor. The intention is to articulate the vision and to influence priorities through the prophetic and teaching leadership entrusted to us as bishops of the church.

The vision of the Beloved Community is set forth in Isaiah 65. In the Beloved Community, God is actively creating something new. The inhabitants of the Beloved Community are at home, where they have access to that which sustains life, where they are deeply known and where they deeply know others. Those who live in the Beloved Community form a web of relationships with one another, with God, and with the whole of creation that enables peace and justice to reign.

Empowered to love others by the grace of God in Jesus Christ, their thoughts and actions are one in knowing that self-interest is satisfied only when all people are valued and all have enough to live. In the Beloved Community, all participate in work that is significant and meaningful, work that builds up the community. In the Beloved Community, differences are not just tolerated but create a dynamic interaction between the poor and the affluent, the young and the old, the artist and the scientist, the farmer and the manufacturer, the wolf and the lamb. The Beloved Community is what the prophets longed for and what we believe is the yearning of the whole of The United Methodist family worldwide.

We are convinced that it is God's intention that societies be organized in such ways that the resources of everyone are understood as gifts from God for the building up of the entire community. The Beloved Community is to be a visible sign of the body of Christ in the world. It is a community that expresses God's intention that all people be one at heart and experience reconciliation. It is an inclusive human family. It is the cause for which Christ lived and died. The Beloved Community occurs when the church locates itself in places of greatest need and offers the gifts of God entrusted to it, including the distribution of resources so that all have enough.

7. The Transnational Church:
Connecting and Sharing Across National Borders

Are the mainline denominations ready for and able to meet the challenges of globalization? There are several interesting efforts to reshape understandings toward more faithful and effective ministry that transcend boundaries of church and state. Global mission used to be foreign mission, but a new shift may be underway.

The United Methodist Church: A Russian Bishop

The announcement that Bishop Ruediger R. Minor of Russia was elected president of this denomination's Council of Bishops for the 2003–2004 term was a consequence of a self-understanding at work. The United Methodists in the United States do not follow the pattern of most mainline denominations dividing work domestically and internationally. Congregations and conferences in the United States and in other countries are not mission partners, but members of the same United Methodist Church. Except for increased financial costs in getting together, they enjoy many benefits from this understanding of church.

Stated another way, the United Methodist Church in the United States is a unit of the transnational church existing in Europe, Africa, the Philippines, and the United States. This structural arrangement is designed to equip all the member churches to overcome the "we/they" attitudes associated with global mission work especially along the North/South dimension. It may also help in the development of a response to the positive and negative forces of globalization.

The Moravians: A Global Church

Another example is the Moravian Church. The Moravian Church in America makes up less than 10 percent of the Moravian Church across the world. Three out of five Moravians now live in Tanzania and South Africa and about four of every five are Black. In the worldwide Moravian Church there are seventeen provinces; the Northern and Southern Provinces of the Moravian Church in America are two of them.

Evangelical Lutheran Church in America:
Colonialism—Accompaniment

The concept of accompaniment has increasingly shaped the approach of this denomination's global mission over the past ten years. The concept is an antidote to colonialism and moves beyond "partnership," which may mask an "unequal yoking of a supposedly powerful giver and a weaker receiver." Accompaniment is "walking together in solidarity that practices interdependence and mutuality." Accompaniment emphasizes "relationship before resources." It emphasizes mutual respect.

> The conversation is no longer between a giver and a receiver but between two churches, each of which has gifts to give and to receive. The difference in kinds of gifts is not prioritized. Mutual respect also applies to regions. In accompaniment each church has the primary responsibility for mission in its area. In conversations between the

churches, each will describe its gifts for outreach in its own country. A fruitful outcome of the conversation is the discovery of the outside church's gifts that may assist in mission in a church's own country.[6]

Accompaniment means encouraging churches to question and analyze priorities and practices. It means being transparent and to engage in honest and sincere dialogue. It means moving beyond the traditional relationships of the past between North and South. It means involving the churches and agencies affected by a decision in the decision-making processes. And, it means acknowledging that churches will be in solidarity with one another in their weaknesses, struggles, and mission.

The Episcopal Church in the U.S.A.: Waging Reconciliation

This example could be used in three of the other categories of renewal: dialogue and relationship building, deep learning, and embracing pluralism. The Episcopal bishops have been doing theological and biblical study on reconciliation. They also have examined the currency of a ministry of reconciliation in times of alienation and fragmentation.

The title of their study book, which gathered together presentations and reflections, indicates how applicable and timely the bishops consider the theme of reconciliation to be: *Waging Reconciliation: God's Mission in a Time of Globalization and Crisis* (Douglas, 2002). This volume and the discussion within the House of Bishops suggest use of the theme in interpersonal relationships, families, international affairs, peace-making and peace-keeping, ecumenical relationships, increased pluralism in society and the church, relationships among churches in the Anglican Communion, and collegiality within the House of Bishops. In phrases that resonate with the theology of Dietrich Bonhoeffer, Frank T. Griswold wrote in his "Closing Reflections" (Douglas, 2002:235–236) to the House of Bishops meeting on waging reconciliation:

> The events of the last days (September 11, 2001), and indeed some of the seasons in the life of this church, have been and are times of suffering. But suffering, as we have heard from so many of the speakers in the last week, is a process of purification, a narrow door through which one passes in union with Christ to a new place. . . . Not that we seek it [suffering], and not that we romanticize it. . . . And yet, if we live it, in union with Christ, it doesn't destroy us, but in a very paradoxical way it breaks us open. It makes us real.

The Episcopal Church in the U.S.A. is digging deep into their tradition and their own denominational life and practice in order to affect a mission that is God's mission in the world.

8. Deep Learning: Transfer of Learning In and Among Denominations

Do denominations learn? There certainly is no dearth of activity, but are there examples of learning from all that activity? Our interviews turned up five examples of learning we believe are important.

Conversation and Transfer of Learning among Denominations
Augustine drew on the writings of Greek thinker Plotinus, who wrote about the likenesses between things that are the same and the likenesses between things different. Mainliners are different in important and unimportant ways having to do with theology, history, polity, governance, and practice. The overriding common experience, however, of chief administrators of fourteen denominations meeting once or twice a year since 1992 is the similarity of issues, challenges, hopes, and fears. If you walked in on this group, you would be hard pressed to identify who goes with what denomination (unless you know the particular jargon associated with a given church body).

At the first gathering in 1992, the group quickly identified a list of common interests and decided to share information and, hopefully, wisdom about:

• the changing role of the national office
• inclusivity policies, use of quotas and goals
• needs of congregations
• relationships to congregations
• computer networking
• theology, policies, and guidelines related to homosexual persons
• the funding of mission
• the organization and coordination of fund-raising
• the evolution of present structure and proposals for restructuring
• research and planning issues
• assemblies including goals, frequency, ideas
• decision-making on significant and controversial topics
• clergy sexual misconduct
• cost reduction processes

- communication within the denomination
- relation to the public media
- legal matters and insurance
- compensation philosophy

The group continues to share ideas, respond to each other's requests for assistance, and delve into subjects of common interest. A comparative compensation study has been done by nine of the denominations involved. Over the years, it has been possible to glean from the discussion's eight common themes, which cover the major items on an agenda toward renewal:

- building stronger linkages among congregations and middle judicatories and the national office
- sharing funding for the whole mission of the church
- resourcing local congregations
- new evangelism initiatives
- preparing leaders for the twenty-first century
- value clashes (for example, participation and access versus cost saving and efficiency)
- correcting overbalances of structural change toward decentralization and autonomy
- searching for new ways to do studies, research, and evaluation

The last two years, this group has piloted a process for deepening its own meetings through disciplined reflection and dialogue, including online conversations between meetings. David Roozen and Larry Peers of Hartford Seminary (with funding from the Lilly Endowment) have guided the pilot. Groups and meetings come and go. This one has proven its value for over a decade.

Do the Mainline Denominations Have a Future? Yes, if . . .

On September 22–24, 1994, the challenge of the future of mainline denominations was the subject of a conference attended by representatives of eleven denominations. Attenders involved pastors, lay leaders, bishops, presidents, moderators, theologians, and denominational staff. Presenters were the authors of some of the writing being done on the mainlines: James Hudnut-Beumler, William McKinney, Loren B. Mead, Clarence G. Newsome, and Barbara Brown. The interaction was lively and participants expressed gratitude for the opportunity to address the topic head on.

Some observations made by participants include the following:

- Theological work is needed on mission that is larger than the ministry of the local congregation.
- Trust is a growing issue among various partners within denominations.
- Personal, professional, and spiritual renewal for church "bureaucrats" is important.
- The theological and practical aspects of increased diversity and pluralism need to be studied.
- It is important for each denomination to define its distinctive characteristics and identity among the churches.
- The future of the "virtual congregation" must be taken into account.
- More attention should be given to youth ministries.
- The changing role of women in leadership is a major motif in denominational life.

Three possibilities about a way to the future for mainlines seem to emerge:

- Wind down and end their work as graciously as possible.
- Recognize the severity of the situation and develop appropriate responses quickly.
- Become immersed in both reality and hope, erecting signs and symbols along the way, taking faithful and courageous action.

Christian Church (Disciples of Christ): 20/20 Vision

It has become customary for a new denominational leader (bishop, president, moderator) to publish in his or her tenure, a pamphlet or book outlining a vision of the denominational future. These visions are a rich source of understanding and inspiration. They usually treat biblical and theological foundations, denominational history, social context, and strategic direction.

A book by Richard L. Hamm, General Minister and President of the Christian Church (Disciples of Christ) is an example of vision casting and includes a direct address of the topic of this book. Hamm defines his denomination as having the marks of true community, a deep Christian spirituality and a passion for justice. The metaphor of the title serves two purposes, 20/20 as a clear way of seeing and the year 2020 as a horizon for the vision projected. Appendix 1 of Hamm's book is a refreshing and direct attempt to answer the question, "Why Bother with Denominations?" Three answers are given: doing things together, nurturing an ethos, and providing for accountability.

Evangelical Lutheran Church in America: Program Evaluation

Do denominations have a "bottom line?" Researchers often look to membership trends and financial statistics to assess the performance of denominations, but over the last decade, the ELCA has taken a very direct approach to evaluating its work. The efforts are modest, but "outcome" language, adapted largely from the United Way,[7] is taking hold throughout the denominational offices. Programs are evaluated by setting outcomes and identifying outcome indicators. Data is gathered and analyzed, and conclusions are drawn. Learning is shared. Within the ELCA, there are four primary purposes of program evaluation, including: (1) program review and assessment; (2) grant evaluations; (3) issue resolution as part of a problem-solving process; and (4) providing evaluation assistance to ongoing or one-time activities of the church.

9. Embracing Pluralism, Valuing Diversity

Some denominational observers see the embrace of an unsettling pluralism as a major source for pain and joy and as a contributor to the perception of "troubles," if not decline and demise. In 1993, David Roozen and Carl Dudley suggested that denominations deserve a pat-on-the-back for this embrace rather than criticism. "Enough self-flagellation"; be wary of "premature obituaries," they (Roozen and Dudley, 1993:889) warned. Have denominations moved beyond statements to action? Here are some examples.

United Church of Christ: Hidden Histories

Click on to the UCC Web site. Find "About Us," then click "Hidden Histories." You will find a complete book online for individual and congregational use designed to increase awareness of the many histories that make up this denomination, especially those not well known. Barbara Brown Zikimund, the author, states the purpose as "to move beyond UCC historical orthodoxy . . . this book seeks to expand knowledge about the diversity of contemporary church life. It will especially stretch leaders in their understanding of the UCC."

Historical orthodoxy is a reference to the understanding that the UCC is a bringing together of the Congregational, Evangelical, and Reformed traditions. Thus, the frequent reference to the UCC as Congregational, Evangelical, and Reformed (these words appear elsewhere on the Web site). This appraisal, however, according to Zikimund, collapses the history of the UCC into a single official channel, which in turn determines how UCC history is studied, who gets the resources to study it, how movements within the denomination get discovered, and how whole histories are lost.

After an introduction, eleven chapters present eleven histories, the knowledge of which will, according to the author, both disturb and excite. They disturb because they stretch present understandings. They excite by illustrating the "strengths of pluralism."

The eleven "hidden histories" of the UCC cover: the American Indian, antislavery and advocacy, German reformed controversies, American foreign mission activity, German immigration, the involvement of African Americans in early missionary work, deaconesses as pioneer professional women, a German group that never became part of the UCC, the role of Hungarian Reformed people, the influence of the women's organization in mission work, and Japanese Congregationalists in America.

If the mainline denominations need strength to move forward into the twenty-first century, one source may well be the power that comes from greater awareness and appreciation of the not-so-well-known histories of each denomination. Whoever said that diversity was a new idea? It has been there all along, waiting to be brought forth, claimed, and made even more central to what mainline denominations are all about.

Evangelical Lutheran Church in America: Lutheran Types

In chapter 4 we suggested that labeling whole denominations along a conservative to liberal continuum is less than helpful because the characterizations disguise the differences within most denominations. One only need listen to the deliberation on sexuality at assemblies of the ELCA to realize that on the interpretation of Scripture, there seem to be a number of models at work.

A more accurate picture, and one perhaps more helpful for understanding and aiding decision-making, emerges when the differences among members are examined more closely. One such "snapshot" of the ELCA has been attempted by this denomination and included as part of its strategic planning.

Five "types" of ELCA Lutherans are described in a study of "Faith Practices" by the Division for Congregational Ministries and the Department for Research and Evaluation of the ELCA. Descriptions of the groups were not developed theoretically and verified experientially. Rather, they came out of the data as a way to summarize and understand the variety of types of commitment expressed by members. Briefly described, the five "types" include those who take a literal view of the Bible, those who put an emphasis on religious experience, those who believe the church is a major help to them in their daily lives, those who take a more "corporate" view of the church, viewing it as an important part of their lives and of value to the wider society, and those who attend infrequently. The percentages of these groups in the church may be surprising:

• the Literalists (19%)
• the Religious Experience group (22%)
• the Church Helps group (17%)
• the Corporate group (25%)
• the Infrequent Attenders (17%)

These groupings are, of course, roughly hewn and should not be taken literally. These are "ideal types" and are useful as a guide and a reminder that members are not a monolith. These differences should be respected and point to the importance of dialogue and relationship building (see category 2 in this chapter) as incidents of renewal.

A denomination is an umbrella or tent under which a variety of activity occurs and a variety of ways of seeing and experiencing the world are at work. The better the comprehension of these variations, the more common learning and action will have a chance. All five of the types exist simultaneously. All five types worship together and agree and disagree under the canopy of something called the ELCA.

An Observation

This chapter has taken a peek inside mainline denominations for signs of life and hope. Mainline denominations are still at work. There are few signs of panic. These illustrations show a commitment to faithful and imaginative efforts despite an uncertain future. There are dark moments in mainline denominational life but there is little evidence of giving up because the need is so great.

One theme in The Rumor is that mainline denominations, particularly the leadership, "just don't get it." They keep doing "the wrong things" because they don't grasp the gravity of the situation. In our interviews, it was obvious that the leaders do "get it." The religious culture of America is full to the brim with fundamentalist religion and religious individualism. Mainline denominations are working toward a different end. They are going against the tide. Can these groups do better? Of course. But, day in and day out, mainline leaders, pastors, lay leaders, and members move forward with the prayer of the Church on their lips.

Lord God, you have called your servants to ventures which we cannot see the ending, by paths as yet untrodden, the perils unknown. Give us faith to go out with good courage, not knowing where we go, but only that your hand is leading us and your love is supporting us through Jesus Christ, Our Lord. Amen. (*Lutheran Book of Worship*, 1978:153)

7. STYLE AND ABILITY: A WAY FORWARD

S ifting through all the information collected for this book—the literature, the interviews, the studies, and our experience—we discovered four basic styles at work. They represent choices that denominations can make as they face the future. Also, there are several *abilities* that denominations will need to develop if they are to have a future.

Style

We called the previous chapter "Incidents of Renewal" because the examples we described illustrate certain qualities associated with renewal rather than other available options. Reduced to their most basic forms, there seem to be four options to address the existential situation of mainline denominations. They could be labeled *styles,* which in this context does not mean standards of writing as in a style manual, the latest fashion vogue, or style as having a certain flair. We mean, following Webster's definition, "a distinctive or characteristic mode of presentation or expression."

1. The *deinstitutional style* uses the seed-husk assumption. The seed of Christianity will survive, even thrive, without the encumbrance of denominations, the husks. Who cares if they die off? They are imperfect containers anyway. The goal is to keep freeing the seed from the husks. But husks aren't easy to shed. They sometimes hang on and on. Nothing less should be expected from husks. They will restructure themselves or attempt to join other husks (merger) or cooperate (ecumenical activities). Those who opt for the deinstitutional style don't want us to be deceived by these last-ditch efforts. Deinstitutionalists will predictably say, "Who needs an institution?" They tell us that institutions are useless and misguided—even as some of the deinstitutionalists try to subvert or gain control of denominations. They want to break free of the old husks, as if the seed can survive on its own.

2. The second style, *deconstruction*, employs the language of postmodernism as it deconstructs denominations as a relic of the past. The sooner we embrace the future, the better. Institutions may be necessary, but they are a necessary evil, pulling us back into the past. Institutions hold us back. They keep us from embracing the new era— and new is always better. Bonhoeffer critiqued the Confessing Church of his time for being so concerned about preserving the old that it was incapable of bringing reconciliation and healing to the church or the society. We have no problem with a deconstructionist methodology as it is employed in postmodern theory. Deconstruction can be useful in exposing the power of symbols, myths, and "truths," especially as instruments of oppression used by power elites. But this style, with the good intention of ransacking the old so that the new may flourish, finds itself bankrupt very soon. It is expert in taking things apart but has shown little skill in putting things back together. It is easier to win a war than to rebuild a country ravaged by war. Competencies abound when it comes to tearing down but are in short supply when it is time to build up. "No, I am contra," replied a Russian leader active in the disassembling of Communist rule, when later called upon to take a leadership role in the *renewal* of the nation.

3. *Restorationsists*, on the other hand, are ever so hopeful. They spend their energy dreaming about the past—that things will be as they were. They care deeply for the church, like an artist restoring an antique to its original splendor and beauty. But institutions are not physical objects, despite our use of *network, web, body, house,* or other metaphors to describe them. The past is past. It will not return. It can be honored or remembered, but not re-created. And because the past is not present, it is subject to the vagaries of memory. It was never that

good. The 1950s as a golden age of denominations is an example of selective memory. Numbers for membership and money were good, but what about racial and gender oppression? The past is important, but not as a candidate for replication.

4. The fourth style is *renewal*. As the term implies, this style embraces the new but does not walk away from the old. It remembers, in order to retrieve the past in a form that's usable for moving into the future. God lures the church toward the future by both refusing our desires to return to some past and accepting the past with all its deficiencies and strengths. This refusal and acceptance makes the past usable for moving ahead. Renewalist institutions will be found writing histories *and* doing strategic planning, honoring traditions *and* preparing vision statements, unleashing the power of identity *and* undertaking bold, even daring, new mission projects. There is no grand narrative for renewal except the gospel. No grand plans will save denominations. The renewalist style is alert to signs of hope along the way. A "No!" is shouted to self-fulfilling prophecies of death. With as much care and love as the restorationists, the renewalists seek to bring the past forward, honor it, and remember it. God is thanked. But a *new* "Yes" is pronounced to God, who brings forward a new future. Faithful action is carried out. There is a new interaction of identity and mission. Within a denomination's identity are sources of renewal. We describe seven organizational strengths upon which to build (chapter 5). Incidents of renewal can be tried (chapter 6). Mission will interact with identity. If it doesn't, it's the same old same old. That may be restoration, but it is not renewal. Here, as a bridge to the next chapter and our conclusions, we describe some features or characteristics of denominations that adopt the renewalist style.

Abilities: An Able Mainline

The use of *ability*, when referring to what a denomination will need to face the future with hope, is easily misunderstood. We are not proposing a workout program for mainline denominations to develop their abilities. Instead, we are suggesting that five abilities—responsibility, vulnerability, connectability, accountability, and serviceability—open a door to a new future.

Ability is used in two ways in the Bible. Clearly, the emphasis is on the *God who is able to,* as in Ephesians 3:20, "Now to him who by the power at work within us is able to accomplish abundantly far more than all we can ask or imagine," or Romans 16:25, "Now to God who is able to strengthen you according to the gospel and the proclamation of Jesus Christ, according to the revelation of the mystery that was kept secret for long ages. . . ." But ability is also a human capacity. The early church, according to Acts 11:29, collected money for a severe famine, following the model that each should give according to his or her ability. Ezra depicts the development of a building fund following the same principle, giving according to "ability" (RSV) or "resources" (NRSV). As Paul attempted to help the Corinthian congregation with the recognition of various gifts, he listed among them the "ability to distinguish" (RSV) or the "discernment" (NRSV) of spirits. The five abilities that follow are not characteristics of a super denomination arrived at by hyperprogrammatic development; they are what happens in the encounter with God, who is able.

We cast these abilities not as predictions but as clues or hints of abilities that future denominations will require. Using psychologist Robert Lifton's (1976) term for basic processes necessary for human life, these five abilities are *formative* in the sense that they shape denominations as strong communities of identity and mission. The absence or weakened state of these abilities will misform denominations and make them unfit for the long haul.

Responsibility

The ability to respond sounds reactive, even passive. In an age of unbounded self-assertion and proactivism, a call to *response-ability* may sound out of touch—and in one sense it is. But the Christian community is always responding. Bonhoeffer longed for people who could and would respond in his day, when they were under terrible pressure to conform and be obedient to government authority. "Who stands fast?" he asked. His response: "Only the man whose final standard is not his reason, his principles, his conscience, his freedom, or his virtue, but who is ready to sacrifice all this when he is called to obedient and responsible action in faith and exclusive allegiance to God—the responsible man who tries to make his whole life an answer to the question and call of God" (1991:258).

Following what Bonhoeffer wrote about denominations after his two sojourns in the United States, we think he would probably include in a call to greater responsibility:

- *A corrective to the understanding of freedom as the right of the individual to do what feels good to include the promise and reality of the Christian community.* Bonhoeffer saw most Christian theology as too oriented to the individual, with the community as a distant, secondary consideration. He put them *together,* regarding the individual as neither prior to community nor derivative from it.

- *A case for a bolder public witness to society.* Bonhoeffer was concerned that the separation of church and state was degenerating into the loss of the public dimension in favor of personal development. He had difficulty with a sermon he heard in America on the importance of having a horizon in one's life. To Bonhoeffer, that was using God for self-improvement.
- *Argument that denominational cooperation is not optional but necessary.* On the importance of the relationships of the denominations to one another, Bonhoeffer treated such relationships not as an option but as a necessity. God allows the denominations to "find each other." Unity is related to increased ability to operate with faithfulness, integrity, and effectiveness in a free society. For the near future, the strategy of *alliances* mentioned as an example of renewal (chapter 6) may hold more promise than mergers as an expression of unity.

In Bonhoeffer's thought, responsibility was always connected to freedom. Freedom was *for,* not from. An able mainline's future will include responsibility for community, public witness, and unity in greater measure than has previously been true. The denomination of the future must keep alive its ability to respond and not wallow in self-pity. The 3-D literature about denominations—decline, decay, death—can and has diminished their ability to respond.

An able mainline will act, revise, reflect, learn, act again, make corrections, and keep on keeping on—while praying fervently to the God who calls us to responsibility in the midst of uncertainty. An able mainline will carry out its responsibility.

Vulnerability

Strange word for an able mainline! But remember the Lord of the Church had no place to lay his head (Matt. 8:20). Also, the Apostle Paul had the temerity to recommend that the little congregation in Corinth base its test of membership not on the world's wisdom but on the foolishness of the gospel: "Not many of you were wise, . . . not many were powerful, not many were of noble birth" (1 Cor. 1:26). Bonhoeffer sought to convert the marginality of the church of his day into an advantage. "We see . . . from below."

In 2000, the Church of Norway published a study on "vulnerability and security."[1] After the tragic events of September 11, 2001, (its Council on Ecumenical and International Relations) this study attracted more attention than (its members) had imagined, because, contrary to much of the wisdom of the day about security, it lifts up vulnerability as a *desirable* state.

The study is critical of inordinate attempts to obtain total security, not only because of the diversion of precious resources from other projects, but also for encouraging pursuit of the dream that we can never be completely safe. More startling and controversial is the study's claim that vulnerability is closely related to *ethical action*. Being vulnerable apparently increases sensitivity to human need. Seeking security may have the opposite effect of leading to an increase in isolation and emotional distance.

U.S. denominations, by virtue of location, are in the part of the world that holds and wields enormous power and wealth. Given that platform of privilege, it seems more and more important for denominations, as acts of faithfulness and courage, to work themselves into more vulnerability, not less. In the last chapter we mentioned two small examples of Methodists and Lutherans working with and among the poor. An international example of vulnerability is Augusta Victoria Hospital in East Jerusalem on the Mount of Olives. Support in the form of money, advocacy, education, and prayer pour in from churches and agencies around the world. The Lutheran World Federation supports the hospital, which has served Palestinian refugees with quality medical care for fifty years as a part of its service ministry, in solidarity with one of its member churches, the Evangelical Lutheran Church in Jerusalem. As a business, the hospital makes no sense. It is vulnerable politically and financially, while serving the most vulnerable among the Palestinian population. No one is turned away.

As mainline denominations take on more vulnerable endeavors, several changes might occur. Mainline denominations may be more attractive to unchurched people as they act contrary to the world's wisdom about security and vulnerability. Second, mainline leaders and members may become greatly inspired and excited about courageous acts of ministry that are consistent with their identity and mission. In turn, they will discover new and imaginative ways to serve in the world.

Also, mainline denominations would serve as a reminder that true security is not found in force or in mad pursuits to control others. "Let not your hearts be troubled; believe in God, believe also in me" (John 14:1), said the Vulnerable One.

Connectability

Mainline denominations that last will have the ability to connect. *Connect-ability* has at least five dimensions. *Community building*, one of the strengths identified in the studies of organizations that last, will connect denominational members in meaningful ways. An emphasis on community will be made in the face of the pervasive individualism in American society and denominations. The triumph of the heartfelt must be tempered with the healing that community brings as people are connected around identity and mission. Other connectability dimensions include the *internal connecting* of leaders and members, old-timers and newcomers, children, youth, and adults—deliberate attempts to span categories of age, gender, ethnicity, and clergy-lay; *external connecting* with other denominations, institutions, groups, international partners, ecumenical contacts, and governments; *use of communication tools* such as newsletters, identity pieces, radio, television, drama; and such newer technologies as Web sites, e-mail, online meetings, and audio and video conferencing; and *dialogue opportunities* for people of unlike minds to pursue understanding—and maybe appreciation and consensus—where there are deeply felt differences.

Accountability

None of the five abilities is more pertinent than this one. The mainline denomination that does not include accountability in today's climate of reports of sexual abuse by church leaders, CEOs ransacking corporations, and the government's managing of news is behind even before the race toward effective and faithful mission even begins.

Accountability has to do with power, and the common wisdom is that no one will easily give up power. But sometimes people do. One of us is a pastor in a mainline denomination. To be a pastor in this particular community of faith, one places oneself *under* authority. A pastor is not the Lone Ranger or lord of a feudal empire, but a participant in an accountability system. The ELCA describes its accountability principle this way: "Leaders in this church will recognize their accountability to the Triune God, to the whole Church, to each other, and to the organization of this church in which they have been asked to serve" (ELCA Constitution, 5.01.h.).

In a world of financial off-shore deals designed to hide debt and inflate income statements, where freedom is understood as the absence of accountability, appropriate accountability may be attractive to outsiders. A denomination with self-imposed accountability practices may receive attention due to its open, top-of-the-table, nothing-to-hide approach.

Accountability is one of those relationships that is different from support, advice giving, or even friendship. It has an element of enforcement. There are consequences for the abuse of accountability.

What can able mainline denominations do to exercise this ability? Two areas seem absolutely necessary. Financial accountability is obvious, but sometimes neglected. The congregation, classis, district, conference, diocese, or national office that is not scrupulous about gathering, storing, and spending money is inviting trouble. There should be regular audits by outside firms, clear reports to governing bodies, and conservative management of resources. It is not unusual to discover that one source of church conflict is over the accountability of funds. The impact on the leadership of a mainline denomination whose national treasurer embezzled funds is one of the case studies in a forthcoming book on denominations.[2] Financial accountability does not guarantee faithful and effective mission, but lack of it is sure to become an obstacle.

Leadership accountability is a second way of strengthening overall accountability. Setting terms of service, performance appraisals, and standards for leadership performance are all ways to increase accountability. The style of leadership is also important. "Command and control" is no longer effective in any setting, much less the church. New ways of leading—with accountability based on full disclosure, consultation, and basic respect for others—must be used.

Policies and procedures related to sexual abuse and misconduct by leaders are not optional. They can be consistent with the religious system, its values, principles, and theologies, but they must also be legally sound while protecting both the victims and those accused. This is no small order. The mainline denominations, after slow starts, have, over the last two decades, been working hard in this area and making significant progress.

Serviceability

The Christian tradition of service is wide, deep, and noble. The New Testament word *diakonia* is the root of diaconate or deacon(ness), denoting a long line of servants of Christ who take on special tasks in church and society, often with the poor, those suffering injustice, and those with ailments of the mind and body. So what is new? To say that the mainline denominations which last will have serviceability seems to require of denominations that which they already do.

In his analysis of postmodernism as the stage on which we all will play, like it or not, Paul Lakeland (1997:106) claims that "the stress on a leadership of service is particularly valuable, when what we are trying to do is to understand how to negotiate a role for Christian community in a radically pluralistic, political, cultural and religious world."

An implication of serviceability may well call for some restructuring of mainline denominations at every level to include external as well as internal leaders, that is, those who represent the church to the world as well as those who build up the community of faith. That may sound like the 1960s revisited (church-in-the-world) or another program for the ministry of the laity in the world. But those emphases have largely been passed over, and they never really found a home in mainline denominations, despite considerable rhetoric to the contrary.

One example of how this might look includes a congregational coordinator of gifts who matches needs or tasks with members' talents for *community* as well as congregational tasks. Members become involved in solving real problems in the local community.

Writing from prison during the last two years of his life, Bonhoeffer imagined a church for Others following Christ, the Man for Others. He hoped for a community of faith that engaged the world at its points of strength rather than exploit its weaknesses. He wanted a Christianity that addressed the world in its adulthood. He suggested that such a Christianity and such a church would experience God's transcendence, not in otherworldly or abstract notions but in "existence for others." "The transcendence is not infinite and unattainable tasks, but the neighbor who is within reach in any given situation" (Bonhoeffer, 1991:274). In Bonhoeffer's vision of the future, he saw a church with serviceability. An earlier translation of his assessment "After Ten Years" (Bonhoeffer, 1953:148), given to friends and family at the end of 1942, uses "Are We Still Serviceable?" as the heading of the last section. It is still a pertinent question to the mainline denominations. This ability has to do with an extreme makeover, not of face and form but of spirit and truth. The mainline denomination of the future will highly value Jesus's words that "the Son of Man came not to be served but to serve" (Matt. 20:28 NRSV). Then, maybe—just maybe—the Church for Others will resemble the Christ for Others.

8. TOWARD THE NEXT RUMOR: FINDINGS, WORRIES, STRATEGIES

It is safest to grasp the concept of the postmodern as an attempt to think the present historically in an age that has forgotten how to think historically in the first place.
—Fredric Jameson, 1991

In gratitude I achieve the right relation to my past. In it the past becomes useful for the present.
—Dietrich Bonhoeffer, in Bethge, 2004

A venerable teacher of preaching, H. Grady Davis, would ask, after a fledgling seminary student's sermon, the provocative question, "So what?" We have arrived at that moment in this endeavor to chase down The Rumor. So what are the implications of all these pages? Here is a summary—findings, worries, and strategies.

Summary of Findings

1. Denominations are a unique North American form deeply rooted in the disestablishment of religion from the state. There are few guarantees of success. They are "voluntary" systems. If they are finished or winding down, new configurations will arise to take their place. However, there is little evidence of that happening. New groupings of persons and sometimes congregations do arise around self-identified issues or concerns. Normally they do not leave the denominations but instead shape a program of co-existence or of resistance and influence.

2. While some denominations have lost members (especially since 1965), that membership loss has slowed. New efforts of evangelism and outreach are widespread. The notion that we are in a post-Christendom age with a residual base of religion or Christianity to build on is widely accepted. It is an open question whether vigorous evangelism endeavors will produce many new members.

3. There is some evidence that denominations which grew in numbers through immigration and the baby boom after World War II are beginning to build new traditions of outreach to the unchurched.

4. Contemporary denominational structures beyond the congregation seem to serve similar functions as they did when denominations were forming: credentialing clergy, conflict resolution, setting doctrinal standards, mission extension (doing together what can't be done alone), setting overall direction, providing pension and health plans. Denominations also developed through a series of stages that are remarkably similar, even given the distinctive features of theology, polity, and history. The various phases through which Methodism evolved in the United States is an example: ethnic volunteerism, purposive missionary association, churchly denominationalism, corporate organization, and postdenominational confessionalism (Richey, 1994). These categories call attention to an inherent tension between denominations as authority systems and agency systems. If the agency system wanes, will authority go too? Or can one function without the other?

5. The denial, comeback, or cynical—no hope options seem to be on the way out with many denominational leaders. Resilience is on the increase. Staring reality in the face combined with large doses of hope, based not so much on "good ole American" optimism as expectations grounded in a faithful, active God, is the option of choice and "the way to work."

6. New ideas are tried all the time but they are seldom evaluated. Specific periodic reviews of programs, policies, and procedures do sometimes occur while attempting to address the effectiveness question.

7. The image that denominations have slid down some steep decline of membership should be tempered with a longer view. This temperance, however, should not be used as an excuse for business-as-usual. Instead, it should be used as a reminder that each age requires its own analysis, evaluation, reflection, and action. The fondness for trends, for "from/to" statements, for "increases" and "decreases," are too general. It is more helpful to face the situation with a healthy combination of reality and hope; erecting signs and symbols along the way, taking faithful action.

8. There exists a comprehensive, in-depth, and mostly positive assessment of mainline denominations. This literature is often scholarly in character and stands as an alternative to the more "popularly" known negative trends. In some cases, the popular literature is apocalyptic in emphasizing decline, decay, and death. But recent assessments that are more balanced exist also.[1] Thomas Frank (1995), at the Candler School of Theology, publicly "swore off" his nay-saying, observing, "the more dire my predictions become, the more popular I became." He labeled this approach "misleading," concluding the negatively generated energy kept church leaders and members from getting at the real work of redefining the role and contributions of mainline denominations in American society.

9. As organizations, the future may be decided by the ability of mainline denominations to engage simultaneously in the tasks of strengthening identity and carrying out lively, effective, mission-oriented action. Mission needs to be consistent with core elements of the identity while paradoxically pushing that identity by creating new places within it for the future. Even core elements may be reshaped or rearranged.

From a theological perspective, this interplay of identity and mission, continuity and change, is expressed in two Bible passages:

Jesus Christ is the same yesterday and today and forever.
—Hebrews 13:8

The wind blows where it chooses, and you hear the sound of it, but you do not know where it comes from or where it goes. So it is with everyone who is born of the Spirit.

—John 3:8

10. Prediction is precarious. There is, however, some basis for the observation that the foundational pattern of denominations as the means for organizing religious work will not change over the next several decades. This is not to say that individual denominations will not change, shrink, expand, readjust. Individualistic forms of religion as well as the disestablishment of religion provided the fertile soil within which denominations grew. Some familiar denominational families will still cluster together and other, more loosely associated church bodies, will continue to be at work.

11. The claim that denominational labels don't mean much anymore needs to acknowledge that, even while they may no longer attend, people still consider themselves Lutherans or Presbyterians. Shifting or reactivating membership normally takes place within denominational families so that when people change, if they change at all, they change within a certain range. The "switchers" may not be loyal to "Lutheranism" or "Methodism" but they are more likely to become Episcopalians than Southern Baptists. The bigger issue for all denominations, no matter where they fall along the liberal-conservative continuum, is the growing number of people who see themselves as religious but have very little to do with *any* organized religious community.

12. The liberal-conservative continuum as a way of characterizing denominations masks the differences within denominations. It seems more helpful to understand the variations under each denominational "tent" by recognizing the differences and developing means for dialogue and common action. Mutual respect and genuine dialogue, however, will not do away with more deeply felt differences. Denominations in the United States are basically democratic systems when it comes to decision-making and when decisions are made in legislative settings, there will be "winners" and "losers." Special care must be taken to address the aftermath of such moments. The goal is to create a positive set of conditions for the "losers." "I had a chance to explain my point of view. I had a chance to be heard and I had a chance to influence others. I didn't like the decision but I will support it for the common good

and the greater mission of the Church, for the unity we share in Christ." Achieving these conditions is no easy task given the polarized atmosphere of good versus evil in American society. Nevertheless, the given of this atmosphere is no excuse for giving up.

13. Let us state the obvious: "Denominations vary in size." Some see "the denomination" as a small center of the activities of the church while others define "the denomination" as all the activities of the church. Put differently, some denominations have a small core—a repository of history, policies, events, and perhaps some services for clergy and church workers like pensions or health plans. Others operate with a much larger core. In others the core is the totality of what exists. See Figure 1.

Figure 1

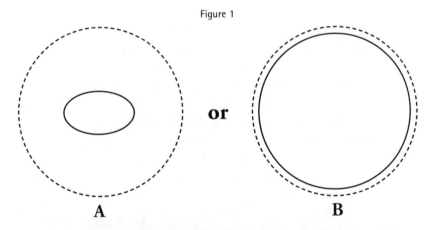

A   B

The solid line represents the denomination. The dotted lines around it are affiliated institutions and agencies or even congregations. For example, in Figure 1A, the American Baptist Churches speak of "cooperating" congregations and "covenanted" regional organizations. In 1972, their "Study Commission on Denominational Structure" (Study Commission on Denominational Structure of the American Baptist Convention, May 1972. pg. 9.) affirmed "that the constituency of the A.B.C. is churches."[2]

Those denominations with a larger "solid line" (see Figure 1B) tend to include congregations, middle entities (presbytery, synod, district, diocese, classis), many institutions like colleges, seminaries, social ministry agencies, myriad services for congregations and support of leaders. The difference among denominations as to what is considered "denomination" is partly determined by ecclesiology. Some claim "All this is church," while others say "The local church is the church. The rest is important, even necessary, because we need each other to do Christ's work. But it is not the church."

If we assume that denominations are not going to change their basic self-understandings and rewrite their histories, is one of the "sizes" of church better suited for the future? We don't believe that one has an advantage over the other in meeting the formidable challenges the future will bring. It may be, however, that those with a smaller core are less likely to lament the decline of mainline denominations because they see the space created as an opportunity to establish a more "networked" church. Some of the prescriptions in the decline of denominations literature (for example, close seminaries) reduce the number of judicatories or do more locally, and so on, are promoted by people already in networked systems. So, they really are saying, "Be more like us."

If the "network" is the organizational shape of the future, we want to note that all kinds of structures can participate. There are, for example, very networked systems within denominations with a larger definition of the church such as the seminary "clusters" in the ELCA. Jessica Lipnack and Jeffrey Stamp (1994:38–49) believe the networked structure does not so much do away with previous organizational patterns as connect them in meaningful ways. In their scheme, the teams, the hierarchy, and the bureaucracy will not so much disappear as be bound together in the network. If this forecast holds true, one future for denominations would be as one of those nodes or as one participant in the network. The smaller circle denominations might have an easier time than the larger circle denominations in adapting to being one node among many. The denominations with a larger core may well try to take too cumbersome a load along to navigate the network.

Some Worries

Despite all our hopefulness and wishing the best for mainline denominations, we are worried about three things: theological strength, the loss of tradition, and the inability to overcome consumeristic forms of religion.

Worry One: Mainline Denominations
Are Theologically Unprepared

Several of the mainline denominations are in the middle of studying and making policy decisions (or not making them) on homosexuality. There have been a variety of study approaches including those based in the widespread participation of members and clergy. Some of the denominations have decided not to proceed with changes in policy; others have made recommendations that have either been defeated or partially adopted. Materials and models for dialogue have been prepared (see category 2 of "Incidents of Renewal," chapter 6).

Throughout the discussion of homosexuality, one impression is vivid: theological competence is weak. We are not talking about the competence of the theologians or teachers who have participated. We are talking about the fact that many of the deeply held and passionately expressed opinions in assemblies seem to have little basis in informed theological discourse. The use of biblical texts, or should we say misuse of biblical texts, is rampant. It often comes down to one side shouting "Do you believe the Bible or not?" while the other side actually appears to look as if they don't.

Past and present attempts to deal with tough issues come to mind. Church historian Mark Noll's (2002b) description of how the Bible was used in the slavery debate is a sober reminder of the track record of many of the churches that now make up the mainline. Noll demonstrates that the alliances formed between American theology and American ideology, which combined to help build the American republic, became the stumbling block on slavery. A kind of enlightened literalism came back to haunt those Christian thinkers and leaders who rode its coat tails for decades. American theology, according to Noll (2002b:445), was unable "to grasp as high as it reached." "It was then neither farce nor irony when the religious habits of mind that have built a Protestant Christian America divided and eventually petered out after the [Civil] War. It was rather a tragedy. . . ." Even among those who evidenced a somewhat different approach to scripture could not or failed to make a dent: "A distinctive Lutheran approach to scripture also remained virtually mute in public discussion" (Noll, 2000b:412). What should have been decided by agreements was decided by armies (Noll, 2000b:445).

This negative assessment of the churches' ability to bring light rather than heat to the question of slavery should cause us grave concern about our current and future abilities. It might be helpful if those trained in theology would occasionally share *how* they do their work along with their conclusions. How do they go about using theology as a resource in approaching real, everyday issues, especially tough ones like war, peace, politics, sexuality, and so on. Dietrich Bonhoeffer could be as abstract as any Christian thinker. He was active in the German academy, but his life circumstances never afforded him the luxury of armchair observation. His faith pushed him toward responsibility in life—deciding, evaluating, and weighing the options. For example, his essay, "What Is Meant by 'Telling the Truth?'" (Bonhoeffer, 1955:326–334) was written while under interrogation by the Gestapo. He didn't want to lie, but he also wanted to lead his interrogators away from family, friends, and co-conspirators in the plot to kill Hitler. Or, read Bonhoeffer's address to an ecumenical youth gathering. Does he bring greetings or crack jokes? There are more important matters at hand. The title says it, "The Theological Basis for the World Alliance" (Bonhoeffer, 1991:98–110).

What is the measure of a theologian? The late Lutheran theologian Timothy Lull could more than hold his own in the academy, but he also chose to write regularly in *The Lutheran* magazine, which goes out to local church members. Lull wrote, until his death, on topics from piety to Lutheran resiliency.

Perhaps there should be a revival of Roman Catholic theologian Bernard Lonergan's project. In 1972 he tried to interest the theological community in linking its research, teaching, and writing to a variety of "operations." His proposal was to be explicit about method, not only the substantive results. Lonergan (1972:6) proposed that theology connect with the various ways human beings operate: "Seeing, hearing, touching, smelling, tasting, inquiring, imagining, understanding, conceiving, formulating, reflecting, marshalling and weighing the evidence, judging, deliberating, evaluating, deciding, speaking, writing." These operations fall into four broad categories:

There is the empirical level in which we sense, perceive, imagine, feel, speak, move. There is the intellectual level in which we inquire, come to understand, express what we have understood, work out the presuppositions and implications of our expression. There is the rational level in which we reflect, marshal the evidence, pass judgment on the truth or falsity, certainty or probability, of a statement. There is the responsible level in which we are concerned with ourselves, our own operations, our goals, and to deliberate about possible courses of action, evaluate them, decide, and carry out decisions (Lonergan, 1972:9).

Lonergan suggested that these four levels were at work in every human endeavor, including doing theology. He recommended that the theologians be: (a) aware of the level on which they were working; (b) clear about the implications of working on that level; and (c) explicit about methods being used, letting the reader in on the how as well as the what. We add a (d): increase work at the judging level (rationality) and the deciding level (responsibility). Time will tell if the mainlines are theologically prepared for the next round of tough questions and issues. We hope so, but the past isn't very encouraging.[3]

Worry Two: That Mainline Denominations May Not Know How to Deal with Tradition

Jaroslav Pelikan (1984), the church historian, reportedly tried to give tradition a good name by making a distinction: tradition is the living faith of the dead while traditionalism is the dead faith of the living. We worry that denominations, like congregations, are being divided into two groups: those who want to hang on to tradition and those who want to "overcome" or "jettison" it. To borrow a Martin Marty (1991) phrase about denominations, "It is deliciously more complex than that." We worry that an "either/or" choice leads denominations into courses of action that are not working because they approach the future as if it had no past. Below are three ways of thinking about tradition based in nonprofit organizational studies, congregational studies, and the Bible.

1. Nonprofits Have Traditionality

There is no more widespread activity across all denominations than planning. These pages could be filled with examples of mainline planning in national offices, middle entities, and congregations. The two of us happen to like planning. We have facilitated quite a bit of it, and even done some research on it. Again, everyone "knows" that good planning, especially of a strategic nature, seeks to match the organization to changes in its environment. A mandatory piece of strategic planning is some sort of context work or environmental scanning whereby the planners try to answer the question, "What's going on out there that is relevant to what we are trying to do here?" But there is research that strongly suggests that, for nonprofits, knowing their place in the environment may be considerably less critical or reliable than exercising the "traditionality" of the organization.

We ask the old catechetical question, "What does this mean?"

a. "Traditionality" is a term used to explain some of the differences between nonprofit organizations and those driven by a profit. Traditionality is characteristic of organizations where continuity is valued. It "originates in a historical perspective in which individuals apprehend present circumstances in light of the past. Individuals rely on patterns of actions and beliefs that were developed in the past to interpret and organize conduct in the present" (Salipante and Golden-Biddle, 1995:9). "Due to the enduring nature of social needs and the importance of public trust, the advocacy-based missions of nonprofits, compared to the profit-based mission of business organizations, call for greater continuity and less frequent and sweeping changes" (Salipante and Golden-Biddle, 1995:4).

b. The sources of traditionality, according to this research, are the "deep structures" which in turn result from underlying and implicit patterns of making choices over time. These organizations come to value core expertise and its continuation, organizational histories which display these patterns of choice, and the ways by which traditionality is kept fresh and current (sounds like a contradiction, given the way we have been trained to think about overcoming tradition or "thinking outside the box").

c. Traditionality is transmitted over time by patterns of practice, not just values. Maintaining core expertise is important because it assures continuity as well as the quality of practices.

d. Nonprofit organizations can make the best use of their traditionality in three ways: (1) by maintaining core expertise and identity through a continuity of practices determining which practices are critical to effectiveness in mission, particularly during "trying times"; (2) understanding and probing their histories: "Stories of past organizational members' effective actions, and ceremonies commemorating key organizational accomplishments, especially in the face of adversity, will encourage the establishment of the proper deep structures" (Salipante and Golden-Biddle, 1995:17); and (3) strengthening their traditionality. Those with formal education and training in management, especially in the for-profit world, are encouraged to "overcome" resistance to change and to provide "aggressive" leadership. Change is seen as a breakdown of "outmoded, traditional practices."

"To the seductive view that effective adaptation must be driven by dramatic changes in strategy and structure should be added the countervailing metaphor of beings surviving due to their fitness, training, inner strength, and character" (Salipante and Golden-Biddle, 1995:16).

e. Three questions become important in the appropriate use of traditionality: (1) What is the mission? What role in society does the organization represent, and how do others see it? (2) What is the core expertise? What is the organization good at doing? Will a proposed change be a natural extension of current practices? and (3) Are the changes facing the organization fundamental, significant, moderate, or minor? Will there be any need for alteration of identity and if so, how far does the organization "stray" (Salipante and Golden-Biddle, 1995:15)?

It may be that, especially for nonprofits, effectiveness is less related to positioning the organization in space (e.g., the surrounding environment) than positioning it in time. Is what we have been a reliable guide to future action? Is our past useable? Is our past, call it tradition or whatever, resourceful or will it blind us to the changes and threats ahead? The concept of traditionality and its uses may at least give pause to the almost universal putdown of the quip, "We never did it that way before." Maybe people who say that are not just warding off changes. Perhaps they are referring to the power in the continuity of practice and the proportionate response to proposed change. Does change call for shifts in identity, in other words, is that us?

2. Congregations as Tradition Systems

Jackson Carroll holds out some hope for mainline congregations. On the basis of studies of "post-traditional congregations," he (2000:98) concludes: "Although most mainline churches will not be able or want to emulate even the somewhat attenuated version of strictness of post-traditional congregations, they can exhibit their own version of seriousness in their ecclesial life. . . ." What does this seriousness look like? Commenting on one example of an "old-line" church in the "rust belt" that is doing well, he (2000:101) observes: "They have not abandoned old practices, but neither do they hold on to them for tradition's sake; they work hard to renew and make their practices vital; and they are willing to innovate. In short, they practice seriousness, not strictness, about the faith and about their congregation's life and ministry." We take Carroll to mean that there are alternative ways to "success." It is possible to have a significant impact without imitating the practices of strict conservative and fundamentalist churches. This alternative is based in knowing one's own tradition so well and having such a sense of it that new practices don't sell out the tradition but renew it. Imitation may be the greatest form of flattery but it is misplaced when it leads congregations away from their traditions and identity.

Carroll recommends "seriousness" while Diane Butler Bass (2000) suggests "reappropriation." Bass sees vitality correlated with the good use of one's tradition, not abandoning it. "Parishes and people must reappropriate tradition, honoring it and reforming it at the same time" (Bass, 2000:144). What makes people free to carry out this dual work of honoring and reforming? Bass's answer is baptism. "By virtue of baptism, churches are bound to tradition but are not bound by it" (Bass, 2000:144).

Nancy Ammerman (2000:302) has also suggested that congregations with strong mainline denominational traditions can find "new life." These congregations, not all, "but a noticeable number are choosing to highlight their denominational particularities." Ammerman reports a change in how denominations are using their traditions to plan for and implement mission and ministry. She (2000:307) concludes that "in about half the congregations interviewed, they exhibited 'an intentional retrieval and construction of tradition' . . . In the midst of a bewildering and mobile world, they (the congregations) have found places to stand. There is an experiment in blending tradition and openness that bears watching" (Ammerman, 2000:207). Seriousness, reappropriating, honoring and reforming, retrieving and constructing, blending and openness—What's going on?

3. Tradition as Memory

Bible scholars Walter Brueggemann and Patrick Miller (2000:60–68) cite examples from scripture that also address conditions that are relevant to the plight of mainline denominations. The title of their study could serve as the title of this book, *Deep Memory, Exuberant Hope: Contested Truth in a Post-Christian World*. Brueggemann and Miller use the "dynamic analogy" of the exile of Israel to make a proposal for the church in a time of dislocation:

• The beloved temple in Jerusalem was destroyed
• The cherished city was burned
• The king was exiled

- The leading citizens were deported and made fugitives
- Public life came to an end

Continuing the analogy, it was for Israel:

- The end of privileges;
- The end of certitude;
- The end of domination;
- The end of viable public institutions; and
- The end of a sustaining social fabric.

In a variety of biblical texts, the authors identify ways to avoid a denial of reality and to go beyond despair (abdicating silence, sensing possibilities). Among the exiles, Brueggemann and Miller discover conversations with God, with each other, with the enemy, with the "strangers" who are, they believe, the "antidotes" to Israel's and our (the church's) situation. These "practices" of conversation offer voices of "sadness, rage, loss, anger, honesty"; of the "voice of holiness" and "order" ("refused to accept the world thin and empty, without God"); "a voice of neighborly transformation," and the "cadences of new social possibility."

The proposal, then, for the church, is that it:

- be attentive to its memory;
- remember its ancient miracles that it continues to treasure;
- have the courage to speak its own cadences rather than the accents of everyone else's language;
- engage old seasons of hurt that are still poignant in their awareness;
- recall its deep incidences against the Holy One; and
- accept its own past life with God.

To what end? To create an "alternative community, deeply placed in risk, summoned in baptism to a world in which . . . God is a pivotal player." "Such an affirmation requires that we church people ourselves be alerted to the vital identity to which we are summoned, for without old baptismal identity the church has nothing to offer and is likely to be a feeble echo of the denial and despair so dense around us." All this comes from "the tradition." The tradition is trustworthy. In it will be found deep joy, quiet confidence, generative resources, and pluralism!

This tradition is immensely pluralistic, not needing to enforce conformity, but instead letting a million voices sound, permitting a million futures to dance before our eyes. It occurs to me that people in charge cannot tolerate pluralism. And so the church, in its cultural dominance, has been a determined vehicle for conformity and coercion. But the church is no longer dominant. This may be the time to replicate our exilic mothers and fathers, who believed that the way into a healed future was to let many voices and many visions play without needing to force all into one" (67).

One is tempted to say "Amen."

So what can we draw from this rich treatment of tradition as memory of what a powerful and loving God has done in our midst? First, there is a remarkable *similarity* of language among our three sources: nonprofit, congregational studies, and significant portions of Scripture. Brueggemann and Miller, for example, call for the church, in dislocated times, "to engage old seasons of hurt that are still poignant in our memories." In organizational terms, the nonprofit studies recommend the probing of organizational histories for "key organizational accomplishments, especially in the face of adversity."

Second, the proposals of Brueggemann and Miller are very much at odds with The Rumor literature. The Rumor literature wants to leave the past behind. In contrast, Brueggemann and Miller find biblical language that is compatible with the witness of the three voices we heard from the study of congregations.

Brueggemann and Miller	Carroll, Bass, and Ammerman
attention to memory	seriousness about tradition
has courage	reappropriates
engages old seasons	honors and reforms
recalls	retrieves and constructs
accepts past life with God	blends tradition and openness

Third, Brueggemann and Miller are reporting on biblical conversations that possess the power to deal with the loss of denominational privilege and the failure of institutions. If mainline denominations have been displaced, then the means for addressing dislocation without falling into denial or despair is recalling, remembering, accepting the past, and sensing the possibilities at hand—those obvious and not so obvious. The answer is not in strategies to regain the center stage, but to engage and serve.

Fourth, in the scheme of Brueggemann and Miller, there is a surprising discovery; namely, that the tradition is so pluralistic. Our guess is that probing denominational histories for stories of strength-in-adversity and competences that overcome obstacles will uncover a rich pluralism rather than conformity. Many voices will be heard again and many visions will be seen again.[4] We would like to call all this the interaction of identity and mission.

4. Renew or Transform?

One overused word in mainline denominations these days is *transformation*. As a concept and set of actions it is often used to debunk "old" ideas such as "redevelopment," "planning," or even "renewal." The word seems to describe a call to go deeper or more quickly than the "older" terms that were based in an evolutionary conception of the world. (Perhaps mainliners, who largely accept evolutionary concepts, are reluctant to embrace revolutionary change concepts so transformation is a nice alternative. At the very least, transformation avoids the political connotation of upheaval.)

The concept of transformation is described in a variety of the leadership and organizational literature. James MacGregor Burns, in his book *Leadership* (1978) and Bernard Bass, in *Leadership and Performance Beyond Expectations* (1985), contrast the transformational leader with the transactional leader. This distinction has had wide influence on the study and practice of leadership. While Bass and others have described many of the ways these two types of leadership are different, they primarily focus on how the transformational leader is a visionary while the transactional leader is a strategist. The latter is very good at moving from A1 to A2; while the former is more about changing A into B with B representing a completely different state of being.

We encounter this language of transformation regularly in church work. There are consultants who write about the "barriers to transformational leadership." There are congregations being served by "transformational" pastors and congregations eagerly searching for one. There are seminaries that have transformational leadership courses or immersion activities designed to be transformational. Searching for a "transformational pastor" using the Google search engine will typically identify over twenty-five hundred different web results.

The word *transformed* appears in the Bible. The best-known example is Romans 12:2: "Do not be conformed in this world, but be transformed by the renewing of your minds, so that you may discern what is the will of God what is good and acceptable and perfect."

The word in Greek for *new* is *kainos*. It means "unused." It is so new it hasn't been used; or something not previously present; or in contrast to something (e.g., old to new with "no criticism of the old implied"). The old has become obsolete; it is time for the new to replace the old like the hymn line, "New occasions teach new duties" (*Service Book and Hymnal*, Lutheran Church in America, 1958:547) or "You call from tomorrow. You break ancient schemes" (*With One Voice:* A Lutheran Resource for Worship, 1995:684).

Perhaps mainline denominations need more renewal and less transformation. We note once again that change involves the past as well as the future, and renewal takes both past and future seriously. We suggest that the danger of overusing *transformation* is in the implication that the past can, even should, be left behind. The past needs to be affirmed as the "base" for the desired future. Every future has a past. The past is the background from which the future emerges. The psychologist Robert Lifton (1976:71) maintains that human beings bring "to bear upon the immediate encounter older images and forms in ways that can anticipate future encounters." Some theorists would go even further, claiming that the future is not only built from older "materials" but that the past itself is reconstructed. Since perfect memory and literal recall do not exist and even the most "objective" historical materials are prepared from some perspective with the use of "selective memory," then the past is never available in original form.

> Instead the individual uses the past as a point of departure and then reassembles those prior experiences together with new inputs and develops all of this in an active ongoing fashion. People build a version of the past just as they build a tennis stroke afresh, depending on the preceding balance of partners and momentary needs of the game. Every time a stroke is built or a memory is instructed it has some originality" (Weick, 1979:49).

Karl Weick (1979:102), a social psychologist, believes a plan works "because it can be referred back to analogous actions in the past, not because it accurately anticipates future contingencies."[5] It is our view that the mainline churches should be about renewal. If transformation occurs, chalk it up to God and give thanks.

5. Tradition Treasures

If tradition is treated in the manner advocated by the sources we have cited, and if identities are mined for buried treasure, those identities and their histories will give three gifts: pluralism, fecundity, and rhythm. There is a tendency to think of pluralism as something new or as a "problem" to be solved. Instead, it is a mark of our past. It should be identified, celebrated, and used as a strong guide to the future. If we can do this, we will learn of all the different ways and different people who have constructed our past. This knowledge, in turn, has the habit of producing offspring or fruit because the identity histories tell stories of accomplishment in time of adversity. The identity histories tell of the ways people overcame, and of the resourcefulness of their traditions. And, finally, all of this takes on a kind of rhythm-the cadence of each denomination as it recovers the past, builds it into a future, honoring and reforming the tradition in ways that produce new ideas and actions.

Worry 3: Carrying Off a Makeover of Consumerism Religion in America May Be "The Impossible Dream"

1. Nobody Can Hear It

Consumption is very appealing. It is a fundamental part of what it means to be American, and the heartfelt, among other things, opens the door to "religious" consumption. At the very least, the heartfelt cuts us loose to pursue our own religious "ends." Heartfelt Americans strive to live in concert with God's plan precisely because they believe that their success in doing so will result in "blessings." It is a church that is less a community of believers doing the work of God than it is a training center where people sign up to learn about God's plan and how to live within it. The worth of religion is thought to be evidenced in successful living. Religion, so conceived, is not a "pact with the impossible" (Caputo, 2001:15), but a means for reigning in and getting the uncertain under control. This sureness and predictability is what people want, and delivering it is an effective church growth strategy. Some churches provide "a universe where everything from the temperature to the theology is safely controlled" (Randall Balmer quoted in *The Lutheran*,

October 2002). It is in this context that we worry about our suggestion that the mainline denominations embrace a different message—that religion is most meaningful and fulfilling when a person lets go of one's self for the sake of, and in the context of, a community. We worry that this voice cannot be heard because of losing the collective ability to hear it. We may have lost the ability to make sense of Bonhoeffer or even the philosopher John Caputo, (2001:14) who writes:

> If safe is what you want, forget religion and find yourself a conservative investment counselor. The religious sense of life has to do with exposing oneself to the radical uncertainty and the open-endedness of life, with what we are calling the absolute future, which is meaning-giving, salt-giving, risk-taking. The absolute future is a risky business, which is why faith, hope, and love have to kick in.

This letting go, as Caputo (2001:31) notes, is directly tied to confessing our love for something else. "Something makes a demand upon us and shakes us loose from the circle of self-love, drawing us out of ourselves and into the service of others and of something to come." But can anyone hear these words?

2. Nobody Will Say It

If it is so difficult to hear these words, why would anyone say them? We could wish that mainline denominations would have taken up the challenge—calling members to look back into their religious traditions for the moments when people were shaken loose from their self-love into the service of others. Being shaken loose makes life unpredictable. Neither have mainline denominations spoken up clearly to turn the heartfelt on its head by issuing a call to be a community that actually lives by faith. But, what if they did? We are worried that our preferred way of being the church is so battered in the current context that mainline churches are giving up or adopting strategies that are more likely to bring in the masses and pay the bills.

We manage to be less worried as we look around more systematically. There is another way trying to be heard, as seen in the work of Carroll (2000), Bass (2000), and Ammerman (2000), described earlier in this chapter. We need more people like these pointing to congregations in the mainline tradition that are serious and growing. At the very least we hope for a large remnant of effective, faithful, and hopeful Christians working together for the benefit of the community. Yet, we have to say over and over again to people who find these words about faith and hope difficult to hear, that it *is* possible.

Strategies: Body Signs

Here is a to-do list for mainline denominations. We have taken the license of talking to the churches as if they were a person.

1. Check Your Attitude

In denial? Reality will catch up with you. In despair? You will miss the rich opportunities God places before you. Try audacious hopefulness. This attitude hopes for a future God has in store.

2. Appreciate and Appropriate Your Tradition

Tradition has a bad name, especially since it has been turned into an "ism." Let's give it a good name by learning how to use it. It should not be abandoned. It should not be "overused." It should be respected and reconstructed. It should be brought forward. In it are three gifts: pluralism, fecundity, and rhythm. It is important to discover these gifts, thank God for them, and use them well. It is a wonderful alternative to chasing every rabbit named "change."

3. Use Your Gifts

There are seven gifts you should rediscover and use. They are a strong core identity, core actions that are "pushy," the free flow of ideas, the conservative management of resources, the building up of community of the faithful, a mission that fits, and an attitude of learning.

4. Do an Ability Checkup

How do you stack up on . . .

> a. Responsibility?
> b. Vulnerability?
> c. Service-ability?
> d. Accountability?
> e. Connectability?

You will need them all on the journey ahead.

5. Think Identity. Think Mission.

You can make two mistakes. One mistake is to do mission without attending to identity. If you take on anything your heart desires, if you have no limits or if you can be stretched and pulled any which way, you will end up dazed and confused. Or, your identity can be static and unchanging. If you just sit there enjoying who you are, if the world doesn't need anything from you, if you just occupy space, the end will come sooner than you think. Now try both. You will learn how well they work together, how well they play off each other. They were meant for each other. They belong together.

6. Scan Your Environment

If you need some good and quick advice, start by reading chapter 10 of David Bosch's *Transforming Mission* (2000) titled "The Emergence of a Postmodern Paradigm." You will have a better sense of what you are facing. You'll make better progress. You can pace yourself. You'll still be around the day after tomorrow neither blown away nor worn out. Lean into the future.

7. Get to Know Your Traveling Companions

Who's in there with you? What do they value? What are their hopes and fears? What do they like (and dislike) about being Episcopalian or Presbyterian or . . . ? Or what about all those different groups within the United Methodist Church? What are they like? Why is pluralism so good?

8. "Modest-ify" Your Programs

You have great ideas. But you try to do too much. Take on less. Analyze what works well and what didn't. Try and try again.

9. Accept Your Structure

Restructuring isn't always the answer. Move more slowly. Look toward strategic, not wholesale change. Your history is reliable, resourceful, and surprising. Don't sell it short.

10. Watch Your Posture

You could get blown over by the strong winds of change. On the other hand, it would be foolhardy to grit your teeth and start running into the wind. You'll end up tired and worn out. It is best to lean into the wind.

The Next Rumor

Rumors come and rumors go. We have, to the best of our ability, tried to chase one down. The chase has been surprising and enlightening. We have covered routine territory and made a series of new discoveries. We have been discouraged and encouraged. We have pointed to some new strategies for the future while we simultaneously worry about it and long for it. As for the next rumor, we hope it is about the mainline denominations still being around doing what they do best—serving as caretakers of the faith while they and it are both reshaped by a God who is actively making the world a better place.

NOTES

Introduction

1. Full report is available from the Department for Research and Evaluation of the Evangelical Lutheran Church in America, 8765 West Higgins Road, Chicago, IL 60631.

2. Full report is available from the Department for Research and Evaluation of the Evangelical Lutheran Church in America, 8765 West Higgins Road, Chicago, IL 60631.

Chapter 1: Conceptual Tools

1. Secretary of State Colin Powell was asked at the United Nations—in response to the United States recommendation to invade Iraq—"What do you want the nations to do?" Answer: "To carefully weigh the evidence, discuss options for response and move forward with action."

2. The authors, the ELCA, and the publisher are strongly committed to the use of inclusive language. The authors trust that this commitment is demonstrated throughout this book. We have retained "mankind" here and some other terms that otherwise are unacceptable today *only* when they are in quoted, historical documents.

3. The *old* Enlightenment refers to the flurry of intellectual activity in Europe in the eighteenth century. Those who were active in the Enlightenment believed they were breaking out of the ignorance of the past. The past, which kept people in the dark with untested and arbitrary religious doctrines, was giving way to the "light" of a new future built on reason and empirical "truths."

4. We are referring to the apparent increasing popularity of religious expression that co-existed with Christianity and predated the Reformation and Enlightenment. These religions are now often grouped together under the banner of neo-pagan. They include, for example, the Druidic religion, based on the faith and practices of the ancient Celtic professional class; Asatru, an ancient, pre-Christian Norse religion; Wiccans, which have their roots in the pre-Celtic era in Europe; and others which follow Roman, Greek, Egyptian, or similar ancient traditions.

Chapter 2: Fragments of Fragments

1. Burkhart (1980) sets out the patterns of centralization from simple "coalitions" to "centralized federalism."

2. The concern about inefficient competition of overlapping national agencies continues today and is often one of the reasons offered for denominational restructuring. For example, see the Lutheran Church in America's restructuring study (1972:33): "Programs and services to congregations and synods are dispersed throughout seventeen agencies. As a result churchwide programs may be fragmented and duplicative. In addition, this number of agencies leads to confusion in the minds of many church members about the distinctive responsibility of each agency and how it services individuals, congregations, and synods in meeting the demands of Christian mission."

3. Research on congregational members' opinions and perceptions almost always turns up some expression of separation or, in more contemporary language, a "dis-connect" between pew and structure beyond the congregation. For example, a 2003 study of Episcopalians "discovered" such a disconnection that was reported in the *New York Times* (August 16, 2002): "In fact, there was widespread indifference to the church's diocesan leaders and national agencies, and little knowledge about what they actually did." Similarly, as the Evangelical Lutheran Church in America (ELCA) discusses declining support for the churchwide organization, church leaders are worried about a lack of connection (see *The Lutheran*, March 2004, p. 44). Why this finding continues to surprise leaders is perhaps the more important "discovery." It should, perhaps, just be accepted as something like DNA and treated as there from the beginning of the formation of denominations in the United States. Then creative strategies can be developed to address it. It is not a new phenomenon.

4. Benjamin Franklin began publishing *Poor Richard's Almanac* in 1733. It was full of sayings that condemned waste (the lack of efficiency) and the value of thrift. Some of these saying are famous, among them "a stitch in time saves nine" and "a penny saved is a penny earned."

Chapter 3: A Bewildering Course of Events

1. Perhaps this is a description of the social side of capitalism that assumes and operates on the same principles.

2. The law gave an individual the right to file a claim against the real property on which the claimant has contributed labor, materials, services, or other value for the improvement of the real estate property.

3. In 1925, John Scopes, a high school biology teacher, was charged with illegally teaching the theory of evolution in a high school biology class in Dayton, Tennessee. His trial received national attention as a battle between "modernists" and "traditionalists." Scopes was convicted but his conviction was overturned by the Tennessee Supreme Court while, in the national media and in the larger society, the antievolutionary, religious fundamentalists were humiliated.

4. Mainline churches also participate in this emphasis. Recent examples include the many prescriptions for evangelism endeavors which lament the denominations' engagement of social concerns like sexuality and ecumenical cooperation as detractors from the "true mission of the church," e.g., evangelism.

5. Elwood's reference to book titles includes Linus Poling's *Faith Is Power—For You,* Norman Vincent Peale's *The Art of Real Happiness,* and Emmett Fox's *Alter Your Life.*

6. The "organizational" problem of personal relationships is that they are nearly impossible to pass along in any systematic way. As a result, it is inevitable that productive relationships,

if they are to last over time (as different people move into and out of leadership), have to move from being based in personality to something that is more formal or institutional. This process is often referred to, following the sociologist Max Weber, as "routinization."

Chapter 4: Numbers

1. These statistics for benevolences are "the amount received from living givers for current official budgets of the permanent Boards and Agencies recognized by the National Body." These statistics were collected in the Yearbooks of the Federal Council of Churches of Christ in America and continued in the Yearbooks of the National Council of Churches of Christ in the United States of America.

2. Hoge, Johnson, and Luidens (1994) dispute this claim.

3. The study was codirected by researchers Carl Dudley and David Roozen of Hartford Seminary, Hartford, Conn.

4. For more information, see *A Field Guide to U.S. Congregations: Who's Going Where and Why*, by Cynthia Woolever and Deborah Bruce. Louisville, Ky.: Westminster John Knox, 2002. The inter-faith project was funded by the Lilly Endowment.

5. The results presented here are based on the responses to the *U.S. Congregational Life Survey*. For the ELCA Lutherans and the Southern Baptists, the respondents were those in attendance at a worship service during the week of April 29, 2001. The Presbyterian results are based on a subset of members and clergy, to be consistent with the long standing Presbyterian Panel. The respective sample sizes are: Lutherans (ELCA)—43,463 members from 420 congregations and 410 clergy from 420 congregations; Presbyterians—587 members and 725 clergy; Southern Baptists—20,000 members from 165 congregations and 124 clergy from 165 congregations.

6. For another view, see Veith (1994), who advocates a return to orthodoxy as a way to contend with postmodernism. He calls it "evangelical postmodernism."

7. We realize this sample size is small, but even if these estimates are off significantly, the number of Southern Baptists *not* taking a fully inerrant position is significant.

8. By and large these questions were not designed to reflect the traditions of the Unitarian/Universalist Association. The responses of the Unitarian/Universalist clergy should be treated in that context.

9. For the UUA, percentages do not total to one hundred because two categories— Unitarian/Universalist principles and world religious traditions—were added to the options for Unitarian/Universalist respondents, but they are not included here.

Chapter 6: Incidents of Renewal

1. See http://www.umc.org/umns/news_archive2003.

2. See, for example, http://www.usoc.org/about_us/getfreport.pdf or http://energycommerce.house.gov/108/action/108-5.pdf.

3. See http://www.organizationdesignforum.org/.

4. See http://www.umc.org/initiative/statement.html.

5. See http://www.umc.org/initiative/pdf/foundation2004.pdf.

6. See http://www.elca.org/dgm/policy/gm21full.pdf, p. 6.

7. See http://national.unitedway.org/outcomes/.

Chapter 8: Toward the Next Rumor: Findings, Worries, Strategies

1. See, for example, *The Quiet Hand of God: Faith-based Activism and the Public Role of Mainline Protestantism* edited by Robert Wuthnow and John H. Evans, 2002. Berkeley, California: University of California Press.

2. This self-understanding of the A.B.C. can be seen as a way to resist the "efficiency" principle which influenced many denominations as they have created and re-created their initial structure over the years. Though he writes mainly about Southern Baptists, James J. Thompson Jr. (1979:47) describes the Baptist mistrust of centralized bureaucratic structures in favor of what he calls "a free-and-easy democracy."

3. An attempt to address this problem of preparing church members theologically for difficult decisions is "Background Essays on Biblical Texts for 'Journey Together Faithfully, Part Two. The Church and Homosexuality'" edited by Arland J. Hultgren and Walter F. Taylor, Jr., 2003. Chicago, Illinois: Evangelical Lutheran Church in America.

4. A congregational example would be historic St. John's Lutheran Church in Charleston, South Carolina. The congregation, which was founded in 1742, finds in its "collective memory": (1) assisting new German immigrants; (2) having once had a pastor banished from the city by the British because he refused to include a required petition for the King of England in the prayers of the church; (3) having a pastor who was America's first military chaplain and was arrested by the British; (4) having once had a pastor who worked with Audubon to publish books on birds in North America; (5) constructing a sanctuary in which to worship that people travel great distances to reach; (6) helping to found a synod, a seminary, and church college; (7) supporting young African American men who became pastors, college presidents, bishops, missionaries; (8) establishing one of the first ministries with African Americans in South Carolina; (9) working to rebuild the city after the devastation of the Civil War; (10) organizing a new congregation; (11) providing lay and clergy leadership for global mission, especially in Japan; (12) rebuilding a church damaged by Hurricane Hugo; (13) having twenty-one of its members enter the ordained ministry and full-time church vocations.

5. Nan Keohane's effectiveness as president of Duke University was attributed to a combination of two factors. On the occasion of her retirement in 2004, observers noted that as she "stuck her neck out" for new initiatives, such as combating excessive campus partying, increasing the number of African American faculty and students, working with an autonomous medical school, creating new programs for women, etc. Keohane, "was the best spokesperson for the idea of one Duke [not an old Duke or new Duke]. That meant building on tradition, building on the past and using that as a foundation to enhance the university in every way" (Duke Magazine, July–August 2004, p. 30).

REFERENCES

Ackerman, Laurence D.
2000   *Identity Is Destiny*. San Francisco: Berrett-Koehler.

Ammerman, Nancy Tatom
1994a   "Denominations: Who and What Are We Studying?" in *Reimagining Denominationalism: Interpretive Essays,* 111–133. Edited by Robert B. Mullin and Russell E. Richey. New York: Oxford University Press.
1994b   *Congregation and Community*. New Brunswick, N.J.: Rutgers University Press.
2000   "New Life for Denominations." *The Christian Century* (March 15).

Bass, Bernard M.
1985   *Leadership and Performance Beyond Expectations*. New York: Free Press.

Bass, Diana Butler
2000   *Strength for the Journey*. San Francisco: Jossey-Bass.

Bellah, Robert, Richard Madsen, William M. Sullivan, Ann Swidler, and Steven M. Tipton
1986   *Habits of the Heart: Individualism and Commitment in American Life*. Berkeley, Calif.: University of California Press.

Berquist, William
1993   *The Post-Modern Organization: Mastering the Art of Irreversible Change*. San Francisco: Jossey-Bass.

Bethge, Eberhard
2000   *Dietrich Bonhoeffer: A Biography*. Minneapolis: Fortress Press.

Bethge, Renate
2004   *Dietrich Bonhoeffer: A Brief Life*. Minneapolis: Fortress Press.

Bibby, Reginald W.
1999   "On Boundaries, Gates, and Circulating Saints: A Longitudinal Look at Loyalty and Loss." *Review of Religious Research* 41:149–164.

Bonhoeffer, Dietrich
1953   *Letters and Papers from Prison*. Edited by Eberhard Bethge. London: S.C.M. Press.
1955   *Ethics*. Edited by Eberhard Bethge. New York: MacMillan.
1971   "After Ten Years" in *Letters and Papers from Prison*. Enlarged Edition. Edited by Eberhard Bethge. New York: Macmillan.
1991   *Dietrich Bonhoeffer: Witness to Jesus Christ*. Edited by John de Gruchy. Minneapolis: Fortress Press.
1996   *Life Together and Prayerbook of the Bible*. Dietrich Bonhoeffer's Works, Volume 5. Minneapolis: Fortress Press.
1997   *Creation and Fall*. Dietrich Bonhoeffer's Works, Volume 3. Minneapolis: Fortress Press.

Bosch, David J.
2000   "The Emergence of a Postmodern Paradigm" in *Transforming Mission: Paradigm Shifts in Theology and Mission*, 349–362. Mary Knoll, N.Y: Orbis.

Brueggemann, Walter and Patrick D. Miller
2000   *Deep Memory, Exuberant Hope: Contested Truth in a Post-Christian World*. Minneapolis: Fortress Press.

Buber, Martin
1958   *I and Thou*. New York: Scribner.

Burkhart, Gary P.
1980   "Patterns of Protestant Organization" in *American Denominational Organization: A Sociological View*, 36–83. Edited by Ross P. Scherer. Pasadena, Calif.: William Carey Library.

Burns, James MacGregor
1978   *Leadership*. New York: Harper and Row.

Butler, Jon
1990   *Awash in a Sea of Faith: Christianizing the American People*. Cambridge, Mass.: Harvard University Press.

Calian, Carnegie Samual
1996   "Building a Visionary Church: An Organizational Theology for the Congregation." *Theology Today* 52:485–494.

Carroll, Jackson W.
2000   *Mainline to the Future: Congregations for the 21st Century*. Louisville, Ky.: Westminster/John Knox.

Carroll, Jackson W. and Wade Clark Roof
1993   *Beyond Establishment*. Louisville, Ky.: Westminster/John Knox.

Caputo, John D.
2001   *On Religion*. New York: Routledge.

Chaves, Mark
1993   "Denominations as Dual Structures: An Organizational Analysis." *Sociology of Religion* 54:147–169.

Chaves, Mark and Sharon L. Miller
1999   *Financing American Religion*. Walnut Creek, Calif.: Alta Mira. *Christianity Today*
2003   February, May.

Cobb, John B., Jr.

1991   *North American Theology in the Twentieth Century.* Article written in August of 1991. See http://www.religion-online.org/showarticle.asp?title=42.

Cochrane, Charles N.

1957   *Christianity and Classical Culture.* New York: Oxford.

Collins, James C. and Jerry L. Porras

1994   *Built to Last.* New York: Harper-Collins.

Davis, Nancy J. and Robert V. Robinson

1996   "Religious Orthodoxy in American Society: The Myth of a Monolithic Camp." *Journal for the Scientific Study of Religion* 35:229–245.

De Geus, Arie

1997   *The Living Company.* Boston: Harvard Business School.

Douglas, Ian T.

2002   *Waging Reconciliation: God's Mission in a Time of Globalization and Crisis.* New York: Church Publishing, Inc.

Douglass, H. Paul

1937   *A Decade of Objective Progress in Church Unity, 1927–1936*, Report No. 4. New York: Harper and Brothers.

Dudley, Carl S. and David A. Roozen

2001   *Faith Communities Today: A Report on Religion in the United States Today* (March). Hartford Institute for Religious Research, Hartford Seminary: Hartford, Conn.: Hartford Seminary.

Ellwood, Robert S.

1997   *The Fifties Spiritual Marketplace: American Religion in a Decade of Conflict.* New Brunswick, N.J.: Rutgers University Press.

2000   *1950: Crossroads of American Religious Life.* Louisville, Ky.: Westminster/John Knox.

Erikson, Erik H.

1958   *Young Man Luther: A Study in Psychoanalysis and History.* New York: Norton.

1964   *Childhood and Society,* 2nd edition. New York: Norton.

1969   *Gandhi's Truth on the Origins of Militant Nonviolence.* New York: Norton.

Finke, Roger and Rodney Stark

1989   "How the Upstart Sects Won America: 1776–1850." *Journal for the Scientific Study of Religion* 28:27–44.

1992   *The Churching of America 1776–1990: Winners and Losers in Our Religious Economy.* New Brunswick, N.J.: Rutgers University Press.

Frank, Thomas E.

1995   "The Rhetoric of Crisis and the Future of Mainstream Protestantism." *Occasional Papers of the Institute for Ecumenical and Cultural Research,* No. 44. Collegeville, Minn.: St. John's University.

Freud, Sigmund

1961   *The Future of an Illusion.* New York: Anchor.

Gaustad, Edwin S.

1989   "The Pulpit and the Pew" in *Between the Times: The Travail of the Protestant Establishment in America, 1890–1960,* 21–47. Edited by William R. Hutchinson. Cambridge, Mass.: Cambridge University Press.

Gay, David A., Christopher G. Ellison and Daniel A. Powers
1996   "In Search of Denominational Subcultures: Religious Affiliation and Pro-Family Issues Revisited." *Review of Religious Research* 38:3–17.

Glock, Charles Y. and Rodney Stark
1968   *American Piety: The Nature of Religious Commitment.* Berkeley, Calif.: University of California Press.

Green, Clifford J.
2000   "Editor's Introduction" in Dietrich Bonhoeffer's Works, Volume 7: *Fiction from Tegel Prison.* Minneapolis: Fortress Press.

Gunnemann, Louis H.
1977   *The Shaping of the United Church of Christ.* New York: United Church Press.

Gusfield, Joseph R.
1963   *Symbolic Crusade: Status Politics and the American Temperance Movement.* Urbana, Ill.: University of Illinois Press.

Hadaway, C. Kirk and David A Roozen
1995   *Rerouting the Protestant Mainstream: Sources of Growth and Opportunities for Change.* Nashville, Tenn.: Abingdon.

Heitzenrater, Richard
1997   "Connectionalism and Itinerancy: Wesleyan Principles and Practice" in *Connectionalism: Ecclesiology, Mission, and Identity* (United Methodism and American Culture, Vol 1.), 23–40. Edited by Russell E Richey, Dennis M. Campbell, and William B. Lawrence. Nashville, Tenn.: Abingdon.

Hoffman, John S. and Alan S. Miller
1997   "Social and Political Attitudes among Religious Groups: Convergence and Divergence Over Time." *Journal for the Scientific Study of Religion* 36:52–70.

Hoge, Dean R., Benton Johnson, and Donald A. Luidens
1994   *Vanishing Boundaries: The Religion of Mainline Protestant Baby Boomers.* Louisville, Ky.: Westminster/John Knox.

Horton, Douglas
1962   *United Church of Christ.* New York: Thomas Nelson and Sons.

Hultgren, Arland J. and Walter F. Taylor Jr.
2003   Background Essays on Biblical Texts for Journey Together Faithfully, Part Two. *The Church and Homosexuality.* Chicago: Evangelical Lutheran Church in America.

Hutchinson, William R.
1989   *Between the Times: The Travail of the Protestant Establishment in America, 1890–1960.* Cambridge, England: Cambridge University Press.

Iannaccone, Laurence R.
1994   "Why Strict Churches Are Strong." *American Journal of Sociology* 99: 1180–1211.

Jameson, Fredric
1991   *Postmodernism, or The Cultural Logic of Late Capitalism.* Durham, N.C.: Duke University Press.

Juneau, Lucie and Joseph Maglitta
1991   "Learning from the Nonprofits: You Think You've Got Budget Problems?" *Computerworld* 25:51–53.

Kelley, Dean M.
1972   *Why Conservative Churches Are Growing*. San Francisco: Harper and Row.
Kirkpatrick, Clifton
2002   *Common Faith, Common Mission: The PCUSA and Its Constitution*. Office of the General Assembly, Presbyterian Church (U.S.A.).
Knudsen, Johannes
1978   *The Formation of the Lutheran Church in America*. Philadelphia: Fortress Press.
Krauth, Charles Porterfield
1972   "The Right Relations to Denominations in America." *Lutheran Confessional Theology in America: 1840–1880*, 101–137. Edited by Theodore G. Tappert. New York: Oxford University Press.
Kraybill, Donald B.
1990   *The Puzzles of Amish Life*. Intercourse, Pa.: Good Books.
Lakeland, Paul
1997   *Postmodernity: Christian Identity in a Fragmented Age*. Minneapolis: Fortress Press.
Lifton, Robert Jay
1976   *The Life of the Self: Toward a New Psychology*. New York: Simon and Schuster.
Lipnack, Jessica and Jeffrey Stamps
1994   *The Age of the Network: Organizing Principles for the 21st Century*. New York: Wiley.
Lonergan, Bernard J. F.
1972   *Method in Theology*. London: Darton, Longman and Todd.
Lutheran Book of Worship
1978   Prepared by the Inter-Lutheran Commission on Worship for the Lutheran Church in America, American Lutheran Church, Evangelical Lutheran Church of Canada, and Lutheran Church–Missouri Synod. Minneapolis: Augsburg Publishing House (American Lutheran Church); Philadelphia: Board of Publication, Lutheran Church in America.
May, Rollo
1969   *Love and Will*. New York: W. W. Norton.
Marler, Penny Long, and David A. Roozen
1993   "From Church Tradition to Consumer Choice: The Gallup Surveys of the Unchurched American" in *Church and Denominational Growth*, 253–277. Edited by David A. Roozen and C. Kirk Hadaway. Nashville, Tenn.: Abingdon Press.
Marty, Martin E.
1984   *Peace and Pluralism: The Century 1946–1952. The Christian Century*. October 24, 979–983.
1991   *Denominations Near Century's End*. Grand Rapids, Mich.: The Stub Lectures Endowment.
Marx, Karl
1978   "The German Ideology: Part I" in *The Marx-Engels Reader*, 2nd edition, 146–200. Edited by Robert C. Tucker. New York: W.W. Norton.
McConkey, Dale
2001   "Whither Hunter's Culture War? Shifts in Evangelical Morality, 1988–1998." *Sociology of Religion* 62:149–174.

Mead, Loren B.

1991   *The Once and Future Church: Reinventing the Congregation for a New Mission Frontier.* Washington, D.C., Alban Institute.

Mead, Sidney E.

1963   *The Lively Experiment: The Shaping of Christianity in America.* New York: Harper and Row.

1987   *The Lively Experiment Continued.* Macon, Ga.: Mercer University.

Mills, C. Wright

1951   *White Collar: The American Middle Classes.* New York. Oxford University Press.

Munson, Howard

1989   "The Nonprofits' Profit." *Across the Board* 26:24–38.

Newsweek

1993   August 9.

Noll, Mark A.

2002a   *The Old Religion in a New World: The History of North American Christianity.* Grand Rapids, Mich.: Eerdmans.

2002b   *America's God: From Jonathan Edwards to Abraham Lincoln.* New York: Oxford University Press.

Pelikan, Jaroslav

1984   *The Vindication of Tradition.* New Haven, Conn.: Yale University Press.

Peters, Thomas J. and Robert H. Waterman.

1982   *In Search of Excellence.* New York: Harper & Row.

Powell, Walter W. and Paul J. Dimaggio

1991   *The New Institutionalism in Organizational Analysis.* Chicago: University of Chicago Press.

Preus, Herman Amber

1990   *Vivacious Daughter: Seven Lectures on the Religious Situation Among Norwegians in America.* Edited by Todd W. Nichol. Northfield, Minn.: Norwegian-American Historical Association.

Regele, Mike with Mark Schulz

1995   *Death of the Church.* Grand Rapids, Mich.: Zondervan.

Richey, Russell E.

1977   *Denominationalism.* Nashville, Tenn.: Abingdon.

1997   "Introduction" in *Connectionalism: Ecclesiology, Mission, and Identity* (United Methodism and American Culture, Vol. 1), 1–22. Edited by Russell E. Richey, Dennis M. Campbell, and William B. Lawrence. Nashville, Tenn.: Abingdon.

Riesman, David

1950   *The Lonely Crowd: A Study of the Changing American Character.* New Haven, Conn.: Yale University Press.

Roof, Wade Clark

1999   *Spiritual Market Place: Baby Boomers and the Remaking of American Religion* Princeton, N.J.: Princeton University Press.

Roof, Wade Clark, Jackson W. Carroll, and David A Roozen

1995   *The Post War Generation and Establishment Religion: Cross Cultural Perspectives.* Boulder, Colo.: Westview Press.

Roof, Wade Clark and William McKinney

1987   *American Mainline Religion: Its Changing Shape and Future.* New Brunswick, N.J.: Rutgers University Press.

Roozen, David and Carl Dudley

1993   "A Premature Obituary." *Christian Century*, September, 27–29.

Salipante, Paul Jr. and Karen Golden-Biddle

1995   "Managing Traditionality and Strategic Change in Nonprofit Organizations" in *Nonprofit Management and Leadership* 6:3–20.

Schmelder, William J.

1997   "A Synod Is Born." *Lutheran Witness* 116 (4).

Senge, Peter M.

1990   *The Fifth Discipline: The Art and Practice of the Learning Organization.* New York: Doubleday Currency.

Service Book and Hymnal

1958   Minneapolis: Augsburg Publishing House (American Lutheran Church); Philadelphia: Board of Publication (Lutheran Church in America)

Sittler, Joseph A.

1962   "Called to Unity. Redemption within Creation" in *The Ecumenical Review.*

Steensland, Brian, Jerry Z. Park, Mark D. Regnerus, Lynn D. Robinson, W. Bradford Wilcox, and Robert D. Woodberry

2000   "The Measurement of American Religion: Toward Improving the State of the Art" in *Social Forces* 79:291–318.

Study Commission on Denominational Structure of the American Baptist Convention.

1972   American Baptist Churches USA, 9.

Thompson, James J.

1979   "A Free and Easy Democracy: Southern Baptists and Denominational Structure in the 1920s" in *Foundations* 1973:43–50.

Tuell, Jack M.

1997   *The Organization of the United Methodist Church.* Nashville, Tenn.: Abingdon.

Veith, Gene Edward Jr.

1994   *Postmodern Times: A Christian Guide to Contemporary Thought and Culture.* Wheaton, Ill.: Crossways Books.

Vision and Expectations: Ordained Ministers in the Evangelical Lutheran Church in America.

1990   Division for Ministry. Evangelical Lutheran Church in America.

Wagner, C. Peter

1999   *Churchquake: How the New Apostolic Reformation Is Shaking Up the Church as We Know It.* Ventura, Calif.: Regal Books.

Waldkoenig, Gilson A. C. and William O. Avery

1999   *Cooperating Congregations: Portraits of Mission Strategies.* Washington, D.C.: Alban Institute.

Wallace, Anthony F. C.

1972   *Rockdale: The Growth of an Early American Village in the Early Industrial Revolution.* New York: Knopf.

Weber, Max

1946   "The Social Psychology of the World Religions" in *From Max Weber: Essays in Sociology,* 267–301. Edited by H. H. Gerth and C. Wright Mills. New York: Oxford University Press.

1958   *The Protestant Ethic and the Spirit of Capitalism.* New York: Charles Scribner's Sons.

Weick, Karl E.

1979   *Social Psychology of Organizing.* Revised edition. Reading, Mass.: Addison-Wesley.

Whyte, William H.

1956   *The Organization Man.* New York: Simon and Schuster.

Wills, Gregory A.

2000   "Southern Baptists and Church Discipline" in *Southern Baptist Journal of Theology* 4 (4).

With One Voice: A Lutheran Resource for Worship

1995   Minneapolis: Augsburg Fortress, Publishers.

Wood, Gordon S.

1993   *Radicalism of the American Revolution.* New York: Random House.

Wright, Conrad

1984   "The Growth of Denominational Bureaucracies: A Neglected Aspect of American Church History" in *Harvard Theological Review* 77:177–194.

Wuthnow, Robert

1983   "Basic patterns" in *Views from the Pews: Christian Beliefs and Attitudes,* 10–32. Edited by Roger A. Johnson. Philadelphia: Fortress Press.

1988   *The Restructuring of American Religion.* Princeton, N.J.: Princeton University Press.

1993   *Christianity in the 21st Century: Reflections of the Challenges Ahead.* New York: Oxford University Press..

Wuthnow, Robert and John H. Evans

2002   *The Quiet Hand of God: Faith-based Activism and the Public Role of Mainline Protestantism.* Berkeley, Calif.: University of California Press.

Yankelovich, David

1999   *The Magic of Dialogue: Transforming Conflict into Cooperation.* New York: Simon & Schuster.